"*A Mighty Change* is a book of hope and hope [It] has made a difference in my life, and I strongly recommend it to others, including the youth .... [It is] enlightening and provides some much needed clarity in a world filled with so many justifications about right and wrong."

—Richard Swanson, School Administrator
Davis County, Utah

"An original winner! Chris Greenwood has given us a great tool to edify and strengthen society! Living the principles in this book has made me a better man!"

—Erik L. Sorenson, President & CEO
Avalanche Marketing Group, LLC

"*A Mighty Change* applies scriptures to our daily lives. [Mr. Greenwood]…will inspire you and help you and your family come closer to our Heavenly Father .... [Y]ou will be blessed for reading it."

—C. Vinn Roos, Manager, State of Utah
Drivers License Buildings, Vehicles, Telecommunications

"Chris has tackled the elephant of sin and broken it down into bite-sized pieces of faith, repentance, humility, and service."

—Jeremy Zaugg
US Military

"Superb! Phenomenal! Thought-provoking! Spiritual! What can I say? This is a book that should be in every LDS home."

—Richard A. Ogden
Production Process Analyst

A Mighty Change:

The Process of Going from Good to Better

By Christopher R. Greenwood

Eborn Books
2011

Eborn Books
175 W. 200 S.Salt Lake City, UT 84101
www.ebornbooks.com

Library of Congress Control Number: 2011926305
Library of Congress Cataloging-in-Publication Data
Greenwood, Christopher R., 1966-
A mighty change: the process of going from good to better /
Christopher R. Greenwood.
        p.   cm.
ISBN-13: 9781890718800

1. Christian life--Mormon authors. I. Title.
BX8656.G75   2011
248.4'89332—dc22
2007049760

Printed in the United States of America

For Tami,
My beloved eternal companion.

"Brothers and sisters, I believe this second part of the journey—this process of going from good to better—is a topic about which we do not study or teach frequently enough nor understand adequately."

--Elder David A. Bednar
"In the Strength of the Lord"
(BYU Devotional Address, October 23, 2001)

ACKNOWLEDGMENTS

This work would not even have been possible without the support and patience of my loving wife, Tami, and our five children, Conrad, Caleb, Collin, Casey, and Calista. Their encouragement and motivation have helped me to reach levels within myself that I never thought possible. They have helped me to raise the bar in my own life to a level where I am unsatisfied with mediocrity and complacency. It is to them that this book is dedicated.

There are others who helped with the manuscript whom I wish to thank as well. Ted Barnes, Steve Dobb, Dick Ogden and Dennis Horne offered significant assistance and were an enormous help in the editing process. All of these people together contributed suggestions, perspective, and insights that were invaluable.

I also wish to extend all my love to my parents and much appreciation to the tremendous priesthood, Sunday School and Primary leaders I have grown up with and worked with through the years. I have also worked with tremendous Young Women and Relief Society presidents who have provided outstanding insight and perspective in my life. Without them, this book would have been impossible. I also wish to thank a thoughtful friend, CM, whose financial contribution made the publication of this book possible.

We all have heroes whom we look up to. People who come into our lives even for a short time who touch us in such a profound way that we never forget them and the impressions they leave with us. They may no longer be with us in this life, but my eternal friends, Con and Ken, had a supreme influence on me, and the lessons they taught me are woven into the fabric of this book. You have not been forgotten!

Above all, I wish to thank my Father in Heaven and my Savior Jesus Christ for providing me with the needed insight, knowledge, and perspective to express my feelings on paper. They have led me by the hand on numerous occasions and have always been there when I needed Them most.

I have tried to the best of my ability to be as careful and delicate as possible with the references and materials presented and to treat them with the respect and acknowledgment they deserve. I, alone, am responsible for the content in this book. Although there are many references quoted by the brethren, and many of their ideas have been used as a template, this work is not an official publication of The Church of Jesus Christ of Latter-day Saints.

Christopher R. Greenwood
Salt Lake City, Utah
October 2010

TABLE OF CONTENTS

INTRODUCTION

A little more than twenty-one hundred years ago, a wise Book of Mormon king named Benjamin on the American continent wanted to know if his people believed the words he had just spoken to them. So he sent messengers out to get a feel for what his people had heard. Although there were many lessons taught by this wise king, one of the more profound scriptures, in my opinion, is found in Mosiah 5:2. It says the following: "And they all cried with one voice, saying: Yea, we believe all the words which thou hast spoken unto us; and also, we know of their surety and truth, because of the Spirit of the Lord Omnipotent, which has wrought a mighty change in us, or in our hearts, that we have no more disposition to do evil, but to do good continually."

The significance and meaning of this single verse have had a profound effect on me through the years. Man is, by nature, carnal. This particular scripture tells me that in order to change my natural disposition, I need to believe the words of the prophet, let their truth manifest itself in me by the Spirit, and experience this mighty change of heart so that I literally don't want to do evil anymore. Is a change like this even possible? How can a person become so converted to the gospel of Jesus Christ that all disposition to do evil is gone? What is the process of change that is involved in going from good to better? What steps do I need to take to have the Lord assist me in this process?

A few years ago, my family and I had the privilege of being members of the Appleton Wisconsin Stake. How affectionately I remember the former stake president, President Stephen R.

Christiansen. Our offices were next to each other at our place of business, and so, from time to time, we would discuss gospel principles and talk about how we could elevate "the natural man" (Mosiah 3:19) to become more Christlike. At that time, it was the objective of his stake presidency to be able to elevate each member of our stake to experience a mighty "change of heart" (Helaman 15:7). I fondly remember how much emphasis was placed on this noble objective and how serious he and his counselors were in attempting to do this.

The Process of Changing

What can occur in our lives and what steps can we take to make ourselves want and strongly desire to experience a mighty change of heart and thereby lose our disposition to do evil?

Some time ago, I saw the following statement written on a conference-room board. Interestingly, I have no idea who put it there or why, but I found the implications eternal – a genuine life lesson. This is what was written:

> *The Million Dollar Question*
> Which is stronger?
> My urge to grow
> -or-
> My resistance to change

I love to ponder this question and ask myself honestly where I fit in according to this statement. When I evaluate myself or when I ponder, I ask myself if I can honestly say that, at that moment, my urge to grow is most dominant. Where do I fit in as a member of His Church and kingdom? Where *should* I fit in?

A scripture from the Book of Mormon, found in 1 Nephi, has helped me to realize that with the Lord's help, and by exercising faith, we can do anything. It says, "Yea, and how is it that ye have forgotten that the Lord is able to do *all things* according to his will, for the children of men, if it so be that they *exercise faith* in him? Wherefore, let us be faithful to him" (1 Nephi 7:12; emphasis added).

Think of the meaning of this verse for a moment. The way that I read this statement is that the Lord is able to do *anything* if He should desire to and if it is according to His plan. Our duty is to have the faith necessary. That's it! Faith! Easier said than done, I know. But how many times have we read this verse and missed the portion about having faith? How many times have we just expected Father in Heaven to fix things and then just expected everything to be okay? We should realize that there is a *high* degree of work involved. We need to do all we can and *then* ask for help in order to raise the bar in our own lives, because, as mortals, we can only do so much. The rest is up to the Lord. The mighty change can occur in our lives if we have the faith necessary to make it happen!

It is my prayer that by reading this book, it may contribute towards the beginning of a desire to perfect ourselves. Along with reading and applying the principles found in the scriptures, may they be the root cause of our desire to go from good to better and experience a mighty change of heart.

CHAPTER ONE
THE CHOICE TO OBEY

Many times as I have taught lessons in my priesthood quorum or Sunday School classes, I have delivered the inspired words of the prophets and explained the repercussions and consequences of choosing not to follow them. Inevitably, someone in the audience will say, "Well, that's nice for you, Brother Greenwood, but most of us are not at that point, yet, in our spiritual development!" Others in the audience will also be shaking their heads in agreement. How can I compassionately respond to such statements? I remember many times praying in my heart to be able to answer this question without offending.

"Who in here has been baptized a member of the Church?" I would ask. As expected, most would raise their hands. "At our baptisms, have we not taken a covenant to always obey Him?" I would query. "Do we not pledge to always remember Him when we take the sacrament each Sunday when we come to church?" Most would miss the point and say that the principles of the gospel are learned "line upon line, precept upon precept" (2 Nephi 28:30). Although it is a true principle that spiritual education does take time and effort to achieve, it is just not the whole picture. We know what is expected of us at our baptism. Therefore, this notion that we are only able to live the gospel principles we choose because we are at a different stage of spiritual development is false. The full text of 2 Nephi 28:30, however, gives a much broader understanding of how we progress in gospel knowledge and testimony: "For behold," it begins, "thus saith the Lord God: I will give unto the

1

children of men line upon line, precept upon precept, here a little and there a little; and blessed are those who hearken unto my precepts, and lend an ear unto my counsel, for they shall learn wisdom; for unto him that receiveth I will give more; and from them that shall say, We have enough, from them shall be taken away even that which they have."

Clearly, in order to have a testimony of a gospel principle, it is first necessary to live it. I firmly believe, as this scripture teaches, that by living a principle ("hearken unto my precepts, and lend an ear unto my counsel") we will gain a fervent testimony, realize the gospel is true, and want to live it. Additionally, the pattern repeats itself: "for unto him that receiveth I will give more." What a fantastic principle! The more you live the precepts, the more you will receive. I believe that the word *receive* implies having the Holy Ghost guide your life and finding out that your life is in accordance with God's plan. Joseph Smith once wrote that it was imperative that each individual should have "an actual knowledge that the course of life which he is pursuing is according to His will" (*Lectures on Faith* [Salt Lake City: Deseret Book Co., 1985], 3:5).

It is a wonderful blessing to know through the Spirit that your life is in complete compliance with what our Father in Heaven wants you to do and become. This blessing truly helps to build the preface to experiencing a mighty change and positions our personal dispositions in complete alignment with His will. This complete alignment will also take away any desire to do evil. As it says in the Book of Mormon: "And they all cried with one voice, saying: Yea, we believe all the words which thou hast spoken unto us; and also, we know of their surety and truth, because of the Spirit of the Lord Omnipotent, which has wrought a mighty change in us, or in our hearts, that we have no more disposition to do evil, but to do good continually" (Mosiah 5:2).

There are many questions that need to be addressed in order for us to tackle the issue head on! For example, why do members of the Church continue to do what they do when they know what they know? Why is there so much complacency or why are there so many "spiritual plateaus" with which some members are apparently so satisfied? Where does this complacency come from? Do these tendencies follow us from the premortal existence? Are these qualities and attributes developed and nurtured in our pre-earth life? Do we have any choice in the matter?

My intention is to be able to answer each of these questions through the subsequent chapters of this book.

Our Own Disposition

Elder James E. Talmage makes an interesting comment in *Jesus the Christ* that helps me understand some of the questions about our own dispositions and character.

> In this struggle between unembodied hosts [in premortality] the forces were unequally divided; Satan drew to his standard only a third part of the children of God, who are symbolized as the stars of heaven; the majority either fought with Michael, or at least *refrained from active opposition*, thus accomplishing the purpose of their first estate; while the angels who arrayed themselves on the side of Satan kept not their first estate, and therefore rendered themselves ineligible for the glorious possibilities of an advanced condition or second estate. (*Jesus the Christ* [Salt Lake City: Deseret Book Co., 1983], 6–7; emphasis added)

According to this text, it is clear that there were some of the spirit children of our Father in Heaven who apparently chose to refrain from active opposition! Is it possible that this same disposition of neutrality can manifest itself today when we choose to be lukewarm (see Rev. 3:16) in our devotion or satisfied in our spiritual development? Taking this idea one step further, Elder Bruce R. McConkie states the following:

> Being subject to law, and having their agency, *all the spirits of men, while yet in the Eternal Presence, developed aptitudes, talents, capacities, and abilities of every sort, kind, and degree* .... As the ages rolled, no two spirits remained alike. Mozart became a musician; Einstein centered his interest in mathematics; Michelangelo turned his attention to painting .... And so it went through all the hosts of heaven, each individual developing such talents and abilities as his soul desired. (*The Mortal Messiah* [Salt Lake City, Utah: Deseret Book Company,

1979], 1:23; emphasis added)

We know that we lived with our Father in Heaven before we came here to mortality. Is it possible then, that the attributes and dispositions developed in the pre-earth life are just mirrored here in mortality? Does this mean that we are spiritually predisposed to complacency? And if so, then how can we overcome this natural inclination?

The intent of this book is to provide you with an understanding of your own divine nature and assist you in bringing to pass a mighty change of heart (see Alma 5:12) which leads to having no more disposition to do evil. It is my intention to provide instruction on overcoming this disposition of complacency through various chapters that discuss ways in which we can lift ourselves to higher levels of spiritual development and assist all our brothers and sisters of the gospel in doing the same. Look, if you will, at this verse from the Book of Mormon.

> And behold, ye do know of yourselves, for ye have witnessed it, that as many of them as are brought to the knowledge of the truth, and to know of the wicked and abominable traditions of their fathers, and are led to believe the holy scriptures, yea, the prophecies of the holy prophets, which are written, which leadeth them to faith on the Lord, and unto repentance, which faith and repentance bringeth a change of heart unto them—
>
> Therefore, as many as have come to this, ye know of yourselves are firm and steadfast in the faith, and in the thing wherewith they have been made free. (Helaman 15:7–8)

Understandably, the path discussed here is not an easy one to choose. It's always more difficult to choose the higher path than it is to follow our own carnal natures and desires. But let's look at this verse of scripture and see how it tells us to go about achieving this change of heart that we are trying to accomplish.

The Key to Changing

In order to change, we first need to be "brought to the knowledge of the truth" (Helaman 15:7). That is the intent of the great missionary work going abroad on the face of this planet. It is part of the mission of the Church. Each one of us, at one point or another, is going to need to be brought to this knowledge of the truth. That is the first step.

Second, we need to "believe the holy scriptures, yea, the prophecies of the holy prophets" (v. 7). How easy it is to be given the truth, but how entirely different it is to *believe*.

One of the most beautiful principles of the gospel of Jesus Christ is the ability to know on a consistent basis not only that the Church is true but also that the individual principles of the gospel are true. For example, I can find out at any time through personal prayer and revelation that what we do in the temples is true, that there is a plan of salvation and that I am of great individual worth.

I well remember an experience on my mission in Australia. While knocking on doors one day, trying to find people to teach, my companion and I were invited into a home where two men and a young woman appeared to be eager to hear our message. We began by asking if we could have an opening prayer to invite the Spirit of the Lord to be present. The response was "no." In our enthusiasm to teach the gospel, we started to teach anyway. What a mistake! How can you possibly teach the gospel without inviting the Spirit of the Lord? After we had discussed several principles of the gospel and had begun teaching about the Joseph Smith story, the investigators stopped us and said they had just received a revelation that they were to have us revoke our testimonies and join their church. They began to mock and ridicule some of the things we do in the temple. My companion and I then bore strong testimony about what we had discussed and promptly left. I was shaken and frightened. My companion appeared unruffled and told me that what they had done had not bothered him. But it had seriously affected me! I was really troubled.

As we traveled back to our apartment, their words kept traveling through my mind. During this time of personal spiritual introspection, my companion got a flat tire on his bike. We would be stopped for a while! I went on ahead a few feet and parked my bike under a streetlight. I sat down on the curb, thinking about what had just happened to us and wondering why I was so scared. At that point, I decided to pray to my Father in Heaven, who I knew from previous experience would answer my prayer. I began to vocalize the feelings of my heart, and I soon felt that wonderful spirit come into my being so powerfully that tears freely fell from my eyes. I *knew* that what we do in the temples is true! Every part of it! The best news is, we can find this out for *any* principle of the gospel. Not just temples or temple work. But any principle!

We are given the promise and the reassurance that we can know at any time the truthfulness of the gospel as long as we are worthy of the Holy Ghost (see 1 Nephi 15:11; 3 Nephi 27:27–28). What a tremendous and reassuring blessing!

So now we know that first, we must be brought to the knowledge of the truth, and secondly, we must believe the Holy Scriptures and the prophecies contained therein. We need exposure and belief! What do these two principles lead to? They "leadeth [us] to faith on the Lord" (Helaman 15:7), our third point. In other words, the beginnings of pure faith! Even with a little faith, powerful things can be accomplished (see Matt. 17:20). The fourth step is repentance, which ultimately leads to our objective, a change of heart. After the desired results begin to take place, we must exercise our faith proactively so that it only becomes stronger. The scriptures say to "repent of your sins and forsake them, and humble yourselves before God; and ask in sincerity of heart that he would forgive you" and then ask that if you "believe all these things see that ye *do them*" (Mosiah 4:10; emphasis added).

What this means is that *knowledge* of the truth + *belief* in the scriptures + *faith* on the Lord + *repentance* = a *change of heart*. This is followed by a lifetime of fulfillment doing the things you know to be true! This is our formula for a change of heart so that we can do good continually, instead of evil.

The Need for Trials and Tribulations

Another interesting point to consider is the fact that in order to have a few first-class experiences, we often must pass through a few first-class trials. It is a fact and part of the gospel that in order to grow we must go through troubled times. We need to go through these rough spots in order to become more perfect and to be able to sit as equals at the same table as Abraham, Job, Moses and Joseph Smith. Trials develop our character and help us on our path to become more Christlike. As the Lord has said, "I give unto you a commandment, that ye shall forsake all evil and cleave unto all good, that ye shall live by every word which proceedeth forth out of the mouth of God. For he will give unto the faithful line upon line, precept upon precept; and I will try you and prove you herewith" (Doctrine and Covenants 98:11–12).

In order to become one of "the elect of God" (D&C 84:34), it is not only necessary but required that we pass through a few of life's tribulations. How does this affect each of us personally? That is a question we will attempt to answer in a later chapter. But it is important for us to realize that without such trials, life would not be a challenge, and it is challenge that determines our eternal home, refines our character, and enables us to become closer to our Father in Heaven. We then need to realize that we cannot continue on this path without the help of our Savior and a complete understanding that He "hath descended below them all. Art thou greater than he?" (D&C 122:8).

I had the privilege of spending a great deal of my adult life in the United States Armed Forces. There are some great benefits associated with life in the military. My family and I have had opportunities that many people don't ever get the benefit of having. Unfortunately, in military life there is the real likelihood that you can be deployed for a possible combat operation anywhere in the world at any given moment. One of the most difficult challenges in my life was the time I had to deploy to southwest Asia for seven months. At the time, my family and I were stationed in Germany, far away from grandmas and grandpas, aunts and uncles, brothers and sisters. I had to leave my wife and children in the hands of the Lord and in the hands of our ward. That was very difficult to do. Not that I didn't trust the Lord or the Ward, but any time I was needed to leave for an extended amount of time to go to an unfamiliar environment for possible combat operations, I had a hard time leaving. My family and I grew much during those long and difficult days, and I feel now, in retrospect, that we became stronger for it. Would I have passed on this learning opportunity if given the chance? Absolutely! But did the experience make me a better person and make my family stronger? I am convinced that it did. I know from firsthand experience the difficulties and anxieties associated with long-term separation. It was an experience I could not have understood without having gone through it myself. The reunion with my family after that long deployment was one of the sweetest moments in my life!

Another principle of the gospel that will help us in our quest to experience a mighty change of heart and have no more disposition for evil (see Mosiah 5:2) is simply to continue to practice on a regular and consistent basis a variety of righteous endeavors whether they are studying, praying, or obeying the principles of the gospel. What you will discover is that eventually those endeavors will become easier to do. A former president of Brigham Young University, Ernest L. Wilkinson mentioned this in a 1963 BYU speech.

> The late President Heber J. Grant was notorious for his comment, "That which we persist in doing becomes easier to do, not that the nature of the thing has changed, but that our power to do has increased." I therefore suggest the more you practice studying, the more you do it, the easier it will be for you to study, and ultimately it will be one of your great enjoyments. ("Lifting One's Sights" in *BYU Speeches of the Year* [Provo, Utah: Brigham Young University, October 1, 1963], 5)

Here's an example of this. One of the things I hated doing most of all while I was serving in the military was jogging. I'm built more for comfort than for speed! But with consistent practice and daily perseverance, eventually, jogging became easier to do. My endurance increased significantly so that it became easier to do.

The Mighty Change

Bringing about a change of heart takes diligent work, but in the end the reward will be greater than any of us can understand. If you want to have a different disposition, remember the words of President Heber J. Grant. In a society where we can have just about anything now, one of the greatest challenges we face is to learn that a Christlike disposition and a change of heart will not happen overnight. But it will happen! You first need to want it! The Savior has promised us the following:

> And now I go unto the Father. And verily I say unto you, whatsoever things ye shall ask the Father in my name shall be given unto you.
>
> Therefore, ask, and ye shall receive; knock, and it shall be opened unto you; for he that asketh, receiveth; and unto him that knocketh, it shall be opened. (3 Nephi 27:28–29)

You first need to recognize what it is that you want and then ask. In this scripture, the Savior wants us to know that if we need something all we have to do is ask in His name. The promise is so deceptively simple and is oftentimes not completely understood. Blessings will only come if we ask and if we make the effort. That is how we grow and develop. Think how boring life would be without any effort or struggle. We would all be stagnant—never growing, never developing, never yearning for something greater, and never finding out just how much we have inside of us to become more Christlike.

Then, *after* you ask, if you are patient, you will begin to experience "line upon line, precept upon precept" (D&C 98:12), a mighty change of heart, and you will receive "his image in your countenances" (Alma 5:14). Alma the Younger explained it this way:

> Did not my father Alma *believe* in the words which were delivered by the mouth of Abinadi? And was he not a holy prophet? Did he not speak the words of God, and my father Alma believe them?
>
> And according to his faith there was a mighty change wrought in his heart. Behold I say unto you that this is all true.
>
> And behold, he preached the word unto your fathers, and a mighty change was also wrought in their hearts, and they humbled themselves and put their trust in the true and living God. And

behold, they were faithful until the end; therefore they were saved. (Alma 5: 11–13, emphasis added)

In the verses that follow, Alma continues, telling us exactly what we need to achieve.

And now behold, I ask of you, my brethren of the church, have ye spiritually been born of God? Have ye received his image in your countenances? Have ye experienced this mighty change in your hearts?

Do ye exercise faith in the redemption of him who created you? Do you look forward with an eye of faith, and view this mortal body raised in immortality, and this corruption raised in incorruption, to stand before God to be judged according to the deeds which have been done in the mortal body?

I say unto you, can you imagine to yourselves that ye hear the voice of the Lord, saying unto you, in that day: Come unto me ye blessed, for behold, your works have been the works of righteousness upon the face of the earth?

Or do ye imagine to yourselves that ye can lie unto the Lord in that day, and say—Lord, our works have been righteous works upon the face of the earth—and that he will save you?

Or otherwise, can ye imagine yourselves brought before the tribunal of God with your souls filled with guilt and remorse, having a remembrance of all your guilt, yea, a perfect remembrance of all your wickedness, yea, a remembrance that ye have set at defiance the commandments of God?

I say unto you, can ye look up to God at that day with a pure heart and clean hands? I say unto you, can you look up, having the image of God engraven upon your countenances?

I say unto you, can ye think of being saved when you have yielded yourselves to become subjects to the devil?

I say unto you, ye will know at that day that ye cannot be saved; for there can no man be saved except his garments are washed white; yea, his garments must be purified until they are cleansed from all stain, through the blood of him of whom it has been spoken by our fathers, who should come to redeem his people from their sins. (Alma 5:14–21)

Doesn't it make sense, then, that a change of heart can affect your disposition? I submit to you that the more righteous a person is, the more he or she is drawn to things of a spiritual nature. Ask yourself whom you are drawn to. Are you drawn to people who genuinely love the gospel, the Savior, and their neighbors? Or are you drawn to people who are more concerned about worldly issues and obtaining worldly fame and fortune? Where do you desire to spend your time?

With the Savior's help, you can achieve a change of disposition. And that change will help you to realize your divine nature and give you a powerful incentive to change even more deeply, more spiritually. Only then will you achieve "a mighty change in…[your heart], that [you may] have no more disposition to do evil, but to do good continually" (Mosiah 5:2). It will take time and discipline, but with the right frame of mind, a positive attitude, and diligent prayer, it can be done!

CHAPTER TWO
THE LITTLE THINGS

Some time ago, after coming out of a meeting at the Church Office Building in Salt Lake City, I decided to go get something for lunch nearby. As I entered the food court, the various smells from all the different restaurants started to make me very hungry. I looked over each restaurant and decided that a slice of pizza was in order. The workers there had just removed a pizza from the oven, and the smell was overpowering to me. I was drawn to it. So were several other people. The sight of the pizza was almost more than I could take. This was the ultimate supreme combination, complete with cheese melting off the sides and many, many toppings. I decided I *had* to have a piece of that pizza. It smelled delicious; it looked fantastic. Almost everyone wanted a piece! I ordered one and quickly sat down at a table to begin my personal feast. The slice was so big I needed two hands to hold it. Enthusiastically, I took my first bite and, after a few seconds, came to a surprising conclusion. It was horrible! I couldn't even finish the pizza. In fact, I threw it away!

As I recall this experience, I can't help but think that sin is much like this piece of pizza. It may look good, it may tempt everyone around you, and it may smell delicious and be almost more than you can take at times, but in the end, it's not as sweet as you were hoping it would be!

As Elder Richard G. Scott once put it: "Have you noticed how Satan works to capture the mind and emotions with flashing images, blaring music, and the stimulation of every physical sense to excess? He diligently strives to fill life with action, entertainment, and stimulation

13

so that one cannot ponder the consequences of his tempting invitations" ("How to Live Well amid Increasing Evil," *Ensign*, May 2004, 102).

Although sin may be enticing and alluring, it does not live up to its expectations. And it keeps us from fulfilling a deeper, more spiritual lifestyle that will, in time, become more rewarding.

How Sin Begins

President Howard W. Hunter once said, "This is the usual course of a man's life as he turns toward evil. First, he is a silent observer, then he becomes a consenting spectator, and finally he is an active participant" (*Conference Report*, October 1964, 107).

How many of us, as we go through our lives and associate with our friends, are actually silent observers of sin? How much sin do we tolerate before we actually stand up and take a position? Do our friends and associates know of our standards and feel embarrassed or apologize when they know they do something we don't tolerate? I think it's important to let others around us know exactly what we stand for. We don't need to be arrogant about it or have the attitude of being "holier than thou," but it is important enough that even the Lord mentions the power of example when He says in the Bible, "Let your light so shine before men, that they may see your good works, and glorify your Father which is in heaven" (Matthew 5:16).

To be a member of The Church of Jesus Christ of Latter-day Saints does not mean to do nothing. We must be active and anxiously engaged in a good cause. The blessings will not come unless we are doing the things we need to be doing. As the Lord said, "men should be anxiously engaged in a good cause, and do many things of their own free will, and bring to pass much righteousness" (D&C 58:27).

What does it mean to be a silent observer, a consenting spectator, and then an active participant? Do these people knowingly watch sin or evil and do nothing about it? How can we as Latter-day Saints avoid the trap of becoming active participants in sin?

While I was going through some military training, I had a good LDS friend whom I will call Zach. Zach was active in his ward. He was a returned missionary and had been married in the temple. He was everything I was looking for in a friend. The man was trustworthy and loyal to his eternal mate. He had two beautiful children, of whom he spoke frequently and whose pictures he had hung in his car and showed to me sometimes in class.

At the same time, Zach befriended another military student who did not have the same beliefs, morals, or principles that he had. Zach saw the popularity of this other student and mistakenly thought that if he were to hang around this guy, he would have an easier time with school and become more popular and become a better military student.

Eventually, what ended up happening was not the plan that Zach had originally laid out for himself. His friend introduced him to a culture and lifestyle that Zach had never been exposed to, and he was led away a little at a time until, finally, he was overcome. Zach was introduced to socializing at bars, which he tolerated. Before long he was going to inappropriate and immoral clubs and literally becoming a "silent observer" of sin. At one of these clubs, he was introduced to a dancer with whom he later became infatuated once she began to pay more attention to him. When Zach's "new friends" suggested they go to this club on a Friday night, he would submit. At this point, Zach had become the "consenting spectator." Eventually, he enjoyed his time spent with his "new friends," and it ultimately led to his destruction. He began to spend more time at that club and with his new "girlfriend." This led to Zach leaving his wife and family, as well as the Church he had loved. He dropped out of school and military training. And unfortunately, despite my efforts to contact him, I never saw Zach again. He had become an "active participant" in doing wrong. And he had become addicted.

I believe that by the time a person becomes an active participant in sin or wrongdoing, he or she essentially becomes numb to any promptings and, without recognizing it, begins down the path that will eventually lead to destruction. It is so important to keep our guard up and never let it drop, because the moment we do, Satan is there with his hosts to bring us down to levels we never thought possible. Satan is cunning, deceptive, and *very* experienced in what he does. We must be constantly on guard. A passage in the Book of Mormon explains this very well: "O that cunning plan of the evil one! O the vainness, and the frailties, and the foolishness of men! When they are learned they think they are wise, and they hearken not unto the counsel of God, for they set it aside, supposing they know of themselves, wherefore, their wisdom is foolishness and it profiteth them not. And they shall perish. But to be learned is good if they hearken unto the counsels of God" (2 Nephi 9:28–29).

A wise person once told me that the chains of habit are too small to be felt until they are too strong to be broken. Satan has centuries of experience. The adversary knows what he is doing. He will not get us to commit murder or adultery overnight, but his plans are so cunning and so subtle that he will gently lead us down the pathway of destruction. Just as spirituality is gained line upon line, precept upon precept, so, too, is wickedness. One thing will lead to another. We must consistently keep our guard up and do all those things that the prophets have asked us to do or we will fall victim to his entrapments. The adversary knows that if he can just get us to be curious about sin so that we want to try it, look at it, or talk about it—whether it is smoking or pornography, for example—we will eventually submit; we will have essentially made ourselves weak in that area, and then Satan can use that to his advantage. He will tempt us where we have made ourselves weakest and get us to sin more and more after that initial contact. And before we know it, we have developed a habit. The safest course of action is just to stay away from evil things to begin with. That way we protect ourselves. President David O. McKay has these wise and prophetic words of advice for us:

> Your greatest weakness will be the point at which Satan will try to tempt you, will try to win you; and if you have made yourself weak, he will add to that weakness. Resist him, and you will gain in strength. If he tempts you in another way, resist him again and he will become weaker. In turn, you become stronger, until you can say, no matter what your surroundings may be, "Get thee behind me, Satan: for it is written, Thou shalt worship the Lord thy God, and him only shalt thou serve (Luke 4:8)." (David O. McKay, *Improvement Era*, July 1968, 3)

16

One of the many things I have tried to teach people and help them to understand as I instruct them in principles of the gospel is that the decisions we make now not only affect our own eternal lives and salvation but also the lives of others behind us. Here's an example. If I, as a father, choose to skip going to Church in favor of going to the beach, or choose not to pay my tithing for one reason or another, the message I am sending to my children and those around me is that the Church is secondary, that it's not as important as my desires, and that I have all the time in the world to do what I want to do because I can repent later. This message we imply with our actions will be taught to our children. And they will transfer it to their children. Chances are, these children will pass this attitude of complacency to their children. Remember, you and I are the only Book of Mormon some people will ever read! Do you realize the implications of that statement? As the Apostle Paul said, "Be thou an example of the believers, in word, in conversation, in charity, in spirit, in faith, in purity" (1 Timothy 4:12).

Somebody is always watching you. Whether they are your children, spouse, peers, coworkers, or even the Lord, many people are anxious to see how you handle certain experiences. A good friend of mine once told me that the true test of a man's character is demonstrated by what he does when he is alone. This is why it is so important that we believe *and* practice each principle of the gospel to the fullest extent possible. You will find that as you do so, the Lord will always bless you for your efforts, because He has promised to! He has no choice in the matter. By obeying Him, we will be blessed. It has been irrevocably decreed, and we know that the Lord is incapable of breaking His own laws. We read in the Doctrine and Covenants that "[t]here is a law, irrevocably decreed in heaven before the foundations of this world, upon which all blessings are predicated—And when we obtain any blessing from God, it is by obedience to that law upon which it is predicated" (130:20–21).

All it takes is a little effort on our end. If we want the blessings, we must make a conscious choice. Nobody else can make that choice for us! The blessings come after obedience to the principles. Satan will do everything he can to get us to fall into one of his traps! Remember, he has thousands of years of experience; he knows what he is doing, and he knows he will be victorious if he can keep you from receiving your blessings.

The Lord has a zero-tolerance policy as far as sin goes. He has said that He "cannot look upon sin with the least degree of allowance" (D&C 1:31). The Lord cannot tolerate sin or any sinfulness in any degree. He is unable to wink at it, ignore it, or turn and look the other way. It is not up for negotiation. This is the way that it is! Many people in the Church, including some friends of mine, seem to believe the idea that the Final Judgment will somehow involve the principle of weighing or balancing with their good deeds on one side of the scale and their bad deeds on the other side of the scale, and if their good deeds outweigh their bad, or if their hearts are basically good and outweigh their sins, then they can be admitted into the presence of God.

Nothing could be further from the truth. Remember the Lord's zero-tolerance policy. This entire process starts with rationalizing little things like "I don't pray every day; I don't feel the need." Heavenly Father would love it if we had a constant prayer in our hearts. He may even like it better than our praying three times a day when our hearts "are far from Him" (2 Nephi 27:25). Another rationalization is that "It's only general conference; I can take the day off. I won't miss anything!" Or how about "Why do I want to improve my obedience? I might not get that promotion at work if people there think I'm too churchy!" Ever heard one of those rationalizations before?

I once knew a young man in high school who, at parties or social events off school grounds, would actually drink from a beer can that he had dumped out and filled up with water! What kind of message does that send to the people who knew he was LDS? Is that something Christ would tolerate? We must begin now to pay attention to these little things. They lead to bigger things. If we won't obey Him in the little things in life—and the Lord knows it— how do we expect to be blessed with the bigger things?

President Ezra Taft Benson put it this way: "As we cleanse the inner vessel, there will have to be changes made in our own personal lives, in our families and in the Church. *The proud do not change to improve, but defend their position by rationalizing.* Repentance means change, and it takes a humble person to change" ("Cleansing the Inner Vessel," *Ensign*, May 1986, 4; emphasis added).

After studying many of President Benson's writings and discourses, I agree that our lives are essentially a culmination of little things that help to create our disposition and character. It is how we treat people in our everyday contacts, how we work, and how we can be trusted that determine the sum of our character. President Benson also said, "Show me a man who *cannot do the little things well and I will show you a man who cannot perform great things well.* Great things are but the composite of little things done well. This means day-by-day attention to little things--to details and relationships" (*The Teachings of Ezra Taft Benson*, ed. Reed A. Benson [Salt Lake City: Bookcraft, 1988], 483; emphasis added).

If we are going to be blessed in life, clearly we need to show the Lord that we are willing to obey Him in *all* things. We don't have the luxury to be able to pick and choose. If we want to be able to have eternal life, there are things we must do and ways we must act. Is it any wonder, then, that the Lord cannot tolerate the least degree of sin? Let's move on toward our next principle of complete obedience.

The Savior has said, "Be ye therefore perfect, even as your Father which is in heaven is perfect" (Matthew 5:48). According to this scripture, we have a commandment to be perfect! The Savior does not say to be perfect some of the time, or part of the time, or even most of the time, but to be perfect all of the time! This is how we show the Lord that we love Him. The Savior has said, "If ye love me, keep my commandments" (John 14:15).

Can We Choose Which Commandments to Obey?

Are we at liberty, then, to pick and choose what commandments we want to follow? Clearly not. How about the words of the prophets? Are things different there? The Lord makes it very clear that when an authorized representative of the Lord speaks under the influence of the Holy Ghost, we are to take that as the literal word of the Lord. The Lord has said, "What I the Lord have spoken, I have spoken, and I excuse not myself; and though the heavens and the earth pass away, my word shall not pass away, but shall all be fulfilled, whether by mine own voice or by the voice of my servants, it is the same" (D&C 1:38).

It is not an option to blow off the words of the prophets. If we are to be true and faithful to the end, part of that responsibility is listening to our prophet leaders. The Lord's will and intention can be determined for our lives through them.

So is it possible, then, that we show our love to our Savior and to our Father in Heaven by what we do and the actions we take? Do not our actions speak louder than our words? Elder Bruce R. McConkie of the Quorum of the Twelve Apostles said at BYU in April 1960 that we spend time with what we love the most. For example, if we love our car more than anything else in this world, we will want to spend most of our time with it. If we love smoking more than anything else, we will want to spend all of our time smoking. Therefore, if we can't gain admittance into the temple because we have a word of wisdom problem, we are essentially saying that through our actions, we love our cigarettes more than we love our Father in Heaven. Strong words, but true words, nonetheless. In a culture where actions speak louder than words, Elder McConkie speaks candidly:

> I think we have a reasonably good standard that we can use to measure the amount of affection and love which exists between us. As such a guide or rule or standard, I suggest this: Time--T-I-M-E. I suggest that the measuring rod for love is time .... *We love the Lord in direct proportion to how much we keep his commandments, how fully and devotedly we do so.* ("Choose an Eternal Companion," *BYU Speeches of the Year 1966,* [Provo: Brigham Young University, May 3, 1966], 6; emphasis added)

In today's time, the same principle and counsel is very applicable. Sometimes rules and regulations or guidelines and standards are disregarded because so many people think that they are "little things" and really don't matter in the whole grand scheme of things. Everything matters! What we say, what we do, how we act! Everything! What Elder McConkie is saying is that our actions speak louder than our words!

Additionally, we need to remember that Elder McConkie and all members of the Quorum of the Twelve are sustained as prophets, seers, and revelators during our general conference sessions. This practice has been in effect since the time of the Prophet Joseph Smith. "The Prophet Joseph Smith asked the people to sustain the twelve apostles as prophets, seers, and revelators" (Roy W. Doxey, *The Doctrine and Covenants Speaks* [Salt Lake City: Deseret Book Co., 1964], 2: 319).

It all begins with changing our thinking process. For example, the scriptures say, "For as he thinketh in his heart, so is he" (Proverbs 23:7). If you want a telestial reward, simply have telestial thoughts. Thoughts equal behavior. Behavior equals action. And our actions determine the kingdom we will inherit. However, if you want to elevate your life to a higher level and achieve the purpose for which we were sent here, you will need to have celestial thoughts, which in turn will cause you to have celestial behavior. Celestial behavior will lead to celestial actions that will take you to the celestial kingdom. *This is the key* to being able to have "no more disposition to do evil" and to experience the mighty change we need to have (Mosiah 5:2). You become what you think. You become whom you associate with. Remember, however, that it takes time and effort (see 2 Nephi 28:30) to be able to achieve a mighty change. It will not come overnight! It will take patience, long-suffering, and wholehearted determination. But it will come, and it will be worth it!

The Word of the Lord

What is the literal word of the Lord regarding the principles that we are supposed to be living today? Are some members of the Church today living on the fringes? Where did the idea come from that it's okay to break some of these less visible commandments as long as you don't break the "bigger" ones? A commandment is a commandment is a commandment! Is it okay to live the standards of the gospel until it becomes difficult to do? Has the Lord provided guidance through His prophets in our day and age on standards of living? Absolutely. There are many commandments that we could discuss at length in this section, but we will only address a few of the ones that most people seem to think are of no consequence.

What has the Lord said about cola (caffeinated) drinks? Has there ever been any guidance in this area? What have our leaders said about it? Elder Bruce R. McConkie says this:

> Obviously the standard of judgment must be uniform throughout the Church, and local officers are not at liberty to add other items to this list [a command to abstain from tea, coffee, tobacco, and liquor]. However, there are many other substances which have a harmful effect on the human body, though such particular things are not specifically prohibited by the Word of Wisdom. *Certainly the partaking of cola drinks, though not included within the measuring standard here set out, is in violation of the spirit of the Word of Wisdom.* Harmful drugs of any sort are in a like category. (*Mormon Doctrine,* 2nd ed., [Salt Lake City: Bookcraft, 1966], 845; emphasis added)

However, you must understand that this is Elder McConkie's opinion. Even though Elder McConkie was an Apostle, in his preface to his book *Mormon Doctrine*, he makes it abundantly clear that he is speaking for himself and not the Church.

So, can we back up his opinion with words from our prophets? Has anyone in the modern day addressed this subject? President Spencer W. Kimball wrote the following about caffeinated cola drinks:

> Wisdom goes beyond the letter of the law. Generally when we speak of the Word of Wisdom, we are talking about tea, coffee, tobacco, and liquor, and all of the fringe things even though they might be detrimental are not included in the technical interpretation of the Word of Wisdom. *I never drink any of the cola drinks and my personal hope would be that no one would.* However, they are not included in the Word of Wisdom in its technical application. (*The Teachings of Spencer W. Kimball,* ed. Edward L. Kimball [Salt Lake City: Bookcraft, 1982], 202; emphasis added)

So we have to ask ourselves, is caffeine as we understand it harmful for the body? Many physicians will tell you that caffeine is indeed an addictive and habit-forming drug that has withdrawal symptoms and everything. My personal opinion is that if it's good enough for President Kimball to avoid, it's good enough for me!

But has the idea of not drinking cola drinks ever been introduced in conference? You wouldn't think so, but in April of 1975, in an official publication of the Church, the following was mentioned: "The leaders of the Church have advised, *and we do now specifically advise, against use of any drink containing harmful habit-forming drugs*" (*Conference Report*, April 1975, 102; emphasis added).

We are left to ask ourselves whether or not caffeine, which is a prevalent ingredient in some cola drinks, is a harmful, habit-forming drug. But the choice is ours to make. However, we need to also remember to avoid even the appearance of evil. There are no double standards in the Church. The Lord was very specific about this when he said to "abstain from *all* appearance of evil" (1 Thessalonians 5:22; emphasis added).

So what is the Lord's word with regard to swearing? Has anything ever been said? President Hugh B. Brown once stated that "[t]he man or woman who is guilty of profanity, swearing, or crude slang unwittingly reveals a soiled mind and a limited vocabulary, and is pitied and shunned by all cultured people. Profaning the name of God is an affront to him, and he has forbidden it" (*The Abundant Life* [Salt Lake City: Bookcraft, 1965], 65). President Brigham Young, in like manner, has said, "Men must quit swearing and taking the name of God in vain; they must refrain from lying, stealing, cheating, and doing that which they know they ought not to do, or they must be severed from this Church and Kingdom" (*Discourses of Brigham Young*, selected and arranged by John A. Widtsoe [Salt Lake City: Deseret Book Co., 1954], 227). Our former President and prophet of the Church, Gordon B. Hinckley has said, "Conversations I have had with school principals and students lead me to the same conclusion—that even among *our* young people, there is an evil and growing habit of profanity and the use of foul and filthy language. I do not hesitate to say that it is wrong, seriously wrong, for any young man ordained to the priesthood of God to be guilty of such" ("Take Not the Name of God in Vain," *Ensign,* [November 1987]: 44).

A few years ago, while serving as a Young Men's president, I chanced upon a young lady who uttered the most vile language I have ever heard at Church or during a Church function. I took her aside, away from the eyes and ears of her peers, and told her that the language she had just used was uncalled for and unladylike. I told her she had a responsibility to hold herself to a higher standard because others were watching her as an example. The discussion did not go the way I had hoped it would. She responded, rather curtly, that she saw no need to stop using that kind of language because her mom and dad used those words, as did her brothers and sisters! I was totally caught off guard by this response! My intent was to show her how others looked up to her and would follow her example. Instead, what I got was a rationalization based upon the behavior of her parents! The same young woman later suggested that we go see an R-rated movie as a combined activity. Is there any question where she got that idea? Remember what was discussed earlier about how the choices we make affect our generation and those following us.

What is the word of the Lord as far as R-rated movies go? Many members I know think it of no consequence if they go and view an R-rated film. They rationalize to the point that they believe a movie containing no sex or nudity is acceptable. If the movie is of historical interest, then it, too, is acceptable. Rationalizations include the fact that they believe that they can handle the violence or the swearing. The scenes will have little effect on them in the long run. President Ezra Taft Benson put it very eloquently when he said, "Don't see R-rated movies or vulgar videos or participate in any entertainment that is immoral" ("To the "Youth of the Noble Birthright," *Ensign,* [May 1986]: 45).

President Benson is very specific here. Like the scripture found in Matthew 5:48 about being perfect, President Benson did not say to see R-rated movies some of the time, or part of the time, or most of the time, but has clearly said not to see R-rated movies, *period!*

For illustrative purposes, visualize the sum of your life on the top of a funnel. Now, as you sin, your life gets closer and closer to that hole at the bottom as the funnel gets narrower. If you watch sugar or some other substance go down a funnel, it appears to get faster and faster as it gets closer to the throat. Sin is much like that. As you sin, doing one thing and then another, you literally get closer and closer to that throat and things appear to go faster and faster until you go down the hole to your utter destruction. In some circles, this kind of negative behavior is sometimes called the "spiral of death." As you plunge downward, it becomes more and more difficult to get control and more and more easy to sin. The rational being "what harm can it do, since I've done all these other sins." However, imagine that you flip that funnel upside down (so that nothing will still fall out of the funnel and that everything you do goes up instead of down.) Now the throat of the funnel is pointed upward, representing that you are climbing up toward higher ground and that as you do more righteous behavior, you get closer to that throat. It becomes easier and easier to do righteous acts. Your own righteousness has created an acceleration similar to a funnel. Eventually, you will go through the funnel to everlasting life.

Although we have only discussed a few of the Lord's commandments, certainly there are many more that we could address. There is no balance in living on the fringes of our faith. You cannot have one foot in the celestial kingdom and one foot in the world. It simply won't work. The scriptures tell us that "No man can serve two masters: for either he will hate the one, and love the other; or else he will hold to the one, and despise the other. Ye cannot serve God and mammon" (Matthew 6:24).

The bottom line is this: if we can't live or abide by the little things, how can we expect to be able to live the bigger things? Don't we show the Lord that He can trust us and show Him our faithfulness by living the little things? We receive the greater blessings that are available to us only after we demonstrate our faithfulness in living the little things.

President Ezra Taft Benson speaks eloquently about living on the fringe:

You have been counseled repeatedly to live in the world, but not be one of the world. *Sometimes some of our members want to live as close as they can to worldly standards and yet qualify for a temple recommend.* Live by the covenants you took in the temple; *do not live on the fringes.* You will be judged by the kinds of movies you attend, by the way you dress, and by the music to which you listen. ("The Gospel Teacher and His Message," Address to Religious Educators, September 17, 1976: Latter-day Tracts [Pamphlets], Salt Lake City, Utah 15; emphasis added)

We cannot be sinners part of the time and saints the other part. Nor can we be servants of the Lord one moment and people of the world the next. Our Christlike character and our development to "do no more evil" stems from step-by-step work, moving from precept-upon-precept growth to application. It blossoms as a result of disciplined and righteous living. We can have that disposition because our Savior has promised us that He stands at the door and waits (see Revelation 3:20). He wants to help us. He will.

CHAPTER THREE
AMBITION IN THE LORD'S CHURCH

A few years ago, I was speaking on the phone to a friend of mine who was in a bishopric in another state and he asked me what calling in the Church I was currently serving. I enthusiastically answered, "I have the best calling in the ward; I am the ward mission leader!" There was a long, awkward pause, and then my friend responded with, "So, when do you think you are going to have an important calling?"

It is no surprise to anybody to know that there are people in the world who measure their success by the type of position they currently have in the Church. It is "the nature and disposition of almost all men" (D&C 121:39) to have temporal ambitions. It reminds me a lot of the man who had an assignment to serve as a Sunday School teacher but decided that particular calling wasn't enough for him. He wanted to be the Sunday School president. Then, and only then, would he be truly happy! Once he became the Sunday School president, he would only be satisfied with becoming the elders quorum president. Then, and only then, would he be happy! Once he became the elders quorum president, he wanted to be in the bishopric! Where does this process end?

Seek Spiritual Gifts

What we really need to do, if we are sincere in our desire to serve the Lord to the best of our ability, is to pray for the gifts of the Spirit rather than seek office. This may be more difficult than it sounds because the gifts of the Spirit are generally invisible to others. In a world

27

that values titles, positions and notoriety, it can be very difficult for some people to seek their true spiritual potential rather than someone else's idea of it. So what can we do about it? How can we overcome this natural and carnal tendency?

Hugh Nibley makes an interesting observation here:

> We are commanded not to ask for or seek for office. Yet nobody seems particularly interested in asking or seeking for gifts, while men constantly plan, scheme, and aspire to office.
>
> Why this craving for office? Because office necessarily has high profile and prestige .... Gifts, on the other hand, are secret and private. (*Brother Brigham Challenges the Saints,* ed. Don E. Norton and Shirley S. Ricks [Salt Lake City and Provo: Deseret Book Co., Foundation for Ancient Research and Mormon Studies, 1994], 436–437)

I remember a time while I was serving my mission when I was assigned by the mission president to take some missionaries over to the airport to fly home. You can imagine their excitement. Interestingly, a few of the missionaries were not excited at all to go home but wanted more time to teach discussions to investigators and follow up with the ones that they had left behind in their areas. They were very excited about the possibility of these investigators joining the Church. At the time, I was a relatively new missionary, and I found these people to be wonderful sources of advice. However, there were others in the car with me who were equally as excited, just for entirely different reasons. I asked one elder what he was most excited for. He told me, "I'm excited to get some lip action that I've missed out on for the last two years!"

Afterwards, as I followed up on what that missionary had said to me, I discovered some very interesting facts. He was unproductive. He was bitter toward the mission president because he had never served in a leadership position, and he was what many would consider to be a "troublemaker" in the various areas in which he had been asked to serve.

My point is this: Before any type of calling to a leadership position can come, we must first be *converted* to what it is we are doing. We have to have a testimony! We need to be an example of the believers (see 1 Tim. 4:12). We need to be humble, meek, and submissive to the spirit and earnestly striving to put off the natural man (see Mosiah 3:19). We believe that this is a Church that is led by true revelation. The Lord *will not* make His intentions known to people in responsible positions who are not *first* doing the things they are supposed to be doing and who are not truly *converted* to the gospel. James Allen has written in his book *As a Man Thinketh* that essentially spiritual accomplishments are literally the end result of holy aspirations. What do we think about when we have idle time or just opportunities to think?

Elder M. Russell Ballard gives some very helpful advice about first showing the Lord that He can trust us in whatever circumstances or trials we are in. These are his words.

> Do not let one day go by when you do not demonstrate to the Lord that you are reliable, that you are trustworthy, that you are dedicated .... *After he has watched you and after you have demonstrated your faithfulness by your service and by your ability to keep your priorities straight in your life, along comes a need for a high councilor, a Primary president, a Relief Society president, a bishop, or a stake president; and the Lord makes it known to the responsible priesthood leader that you are ready because you have lived up to the commitments and promises that you made before you were ever born.* ("You—The Leaders in 1988," *Ensign,* March 1979, 71–73; emphasis added)

A friend once told me that the Lord does not choose the qualified, He qualifies the chosen. I have found this to be very true. One of the most important things we can do in this life is to show the Lord that He can trust us in any situation.

The Call to Teach

Many people in the Church have the belief that calls to a position of leadership somehow make an individual more intellectual, more spiritual, or generally more popular and, therefore, better overall. I remember many missionaries who felt that unless they served as trainers, district leaders or zone leaders, their mission was a failure. I submit to you that a truly converted missionary understands that these leadership roles are nothing more than administration jobs, some requiring numerous hours spent traveling! How burdensome! When a missionary is called, he or she is called to proselytize and to bring souls unto Christ. Proselytizing is the ultimate privilege for which a missionary works, prays, fasts, and aspires; the task takes a great deal of spiritual effort. Imagine working so hard to catch the spirit of your calling and then having to spend all your time administering! There is a significant difference between *administering* and *ministering*. The former is something that needs to happen, but it does not make you any better than someone who is ministering. Is it better to be a teacher and help somebody to understand the gospel of Jesus Christ or to be the administrator over the teachers? There is no greater calling than that of a teacher. Even though these calls to administration can still provide growth and development, teaching is the most important. Let me illustrate the point with a quote from the LDS *Church News*:

> Of all tasks associated with the work of the Lord, teaching could be regarded as the most ubiquitous, the most fundamental .... Virtually everything pertaining to the salvation and eternal life of God's sons and daughters depends upon effective teaching. In the grand mission of the Church—to invite all to come unto Christ and be perfected in Him—teaching is the essence of each of the three dimensions: proclaiming the gospel, perfecting the Saints and redeeming the dead. (R. Scott Lloyd, "A Teacher's Calling comes from the Lord; No Duty is Greater," LDS *Church News* [September 6, 1997], 16)

In a revelation to the Prophet Joseph Smith, the Lord said "Remember the worth of souls is great in the sight of God" (D&C 18:10). We can help people to understand that worth through teaching.

Motives and Hidden Agendas

Some missionaries and other members of the Church begin to think that they have to somehow impress the people who are in positions in order to be called to leadership, as in the "good ol' boys system." Nothing could be further from the truth! If we understand *why* we serve, we aren't concerned about *where* we serve or what position we obtain in the Church. Joseph Fielding McConkie once wrote:

God calls and educates his own prophets. The idea is prevalent that with the call to the prophetic office comes an endowment of spiritual ability, understanding, and power that was not previously experienced and that exceeds that which is enjoyed generally by righteous men. Challenging that conclusion, Elder Bruce R. McConkie has written that a call to positions of leadership "adds little knowledge or power of discernment to an individual, although every person called to a position in the Church does grow in grace, knowledge, and power by magnifying the calling given him." (*Seeking the Spirit* [Salt Lake City: Deseret Book Co., 1978], 33)

Spiritual education is a very difficult thing to achieve and to develop. But principles like the one Elder Bruce R. McConkie is writing about in his book *Mormon Doctrine* take some time to accomplish! This development does not make you any better than the person you lead, nor does it make you any better than anybody else. As a matter of fact, I believe spirituality is not an office. I do not believe that faith is an office one can hold. Wisdom is not an office. These are all gifts given to us by a loving Father in Heaven, but in order for us to be able to use these gifts we first need to develop them. I call these gifts from our Father in Heaven "attributes of godliness." I do not believe that these attributes are entirely contingent upon calls to serve. I do not believe that they are associated with age. Spiritual strengths and the gifts from our Father in Heaven come from doing works of righteousness, not from watching about the acts of others! Remember, in the Bible, one of the books in the New Testament is called the "Acts of the Apostles" not the *resolutions* of the Apostles! In my opinion, the quality in life that is most often faked is spirituality. It is easy to give out appearances that you're spiritual, but remember, bishops and stake presidents are blessed with the gift and power of discernment. You may be able to fool them for a time, but eventually they will know the truth. Most of us will never serve in these positions, but that fact can't stop us from leading righteous lives and qualifying for the most important position—the one on the right hand of the Father.

Having proper motives is not something that is new to Church leadership. We need to be sincere about the type of service that we render. Is there any question about the sincerity of Joseph Smith or Brigham Young? Sincerity is evident in everything that they did! Elder John A. Widtsoe had some very wise council that is even applicable to us in our day. He said the following:

Obedience to law must be impelled by simple honesty or sincerity. I wonder if we are quite sincere in our obedience, or if we give to the Lord with hidden motives in our hearts. We cannot be anything but sincere if we are true Latter-day Saints. Men who give of their time, talents or means without fully giving themselves, their hearts, only give in part. (*Conference Report*, April 1925, 29)

Not all of us are destined to be famous. We can't all be illustrious! The most important work we will ever do is within the walls of our home! There is nothing more important! President Harold B. Lee once said:

I find some of our brethren who are engaged in some leadership positions justify their neglect of their family because they say that they are engaged in the Lord's work. I say to them, "My dear brother, do you realize that the most important part of the Lord's work that you will do, is the work that you do within the walls of your own home? *That is the most important work of the Lord.* Don't get your sense of values mixed up." (Harold B. Lee, "Doing the Right Things for the Right Reasons," in BYU *Speeches of the Year*, [Provo: Brigham Young University, 1961], 5; emphasis added)

The work that we do in our homes will affect generations! Most of us will serve out our lives in quiet faithfulness often with very little worldly recognition. That does not mean that we are not capable of serving in these positions. I spoke with a stake president once who said that, while he was younger, the Spirit whispered to him, saying he was going to be called to be the bishop when the ward reorganized. This scared him and made him reinvestigate his thoughts. Again after much prayer, the quiet whisperings of the Spirit confirmed that he would indeed be called to be the bishop. So, following through on that confirmation, he sought heavenly guidance and chose the people he wanted to appoint as counselors. The problem was that the call never came, and another priesthood holder from the ward was called to be the bishop. Why do you suppose that this worthy priesthood bearer who was told that he would be the bishop was not called? This confused him because he had always considered himself knowledgeable in recognizing the promptings of the Spirit. His Church credentials were impeccable! He was a returned missionary, he had been married in the temple, and he had a valiant testimony of the gospel. He was living worthy of his priesthood. He was a seasoned leader familiar with the promptings of the Spirit. What had gone wrong?

The answer came to him, slowly, but eventually. It occurred to him one day that maybe the Lord was telling him that if the call were to come to him to serve as bishop, that he would be *worthy* in every regard to have accepted the calling. In fact, the Lord was pouring out His love upon him! After coming to this insight, the Spirit bore witness to my friend of his personal worthiness and he was able to move on. The call to serve as a bishop did come eventually, just not in the time or place he had thought. My friend learned the importance of always keeping yourself worthy and continuing to serve the Lord regardless of your position. President Howard W. Hunter said this in his teachings: "We should be willing to serve and grow quietly. If you feel that much of what you do this year or in the years to come does not make you very famous, take heart. Most of the best people who ever lived weren't very famous either. Serve and grow, faithfully and quietly. Be on guard regarding the praise of men" (*The Teachings of Howard W. Hunter*, ed. Clyde J. Williams [Salt Lake City: Bookcraft, 1997], 67).

A few years ago, I discovered the following diagram written on a whiteboard, almost as if somebody had been brainstorming. To me, it clearly explained the huge chasm that exists between means and motives. One path is clearly the Lord's way; the other path is the way Satan would endorse. Let me illustrate.

	Motive	Means	Goal
Christ	God's Glory	Free Agency	Save all souls
Satan	Himself	Force	Save all souls

As I understand this, Christ's motive is God's glory. His intention is to save all souls through individual free agency. Conversely, Satan's motive is himself. He wanted to save all souls through force and manipulation. As I read this on the board, I asked myself if my motives were pure, as Christ's, and if I performed my duties to seek God's glory or if my motives were selfish and for my own gratification. It is important to ask yourself if you are doing things to be seen of men or to further the kingdom of God.

Another issue one needs to consider about positions of leadership, whether they are in the Church or outside it, is the attached spotlight or the constant public adoration and scrutiny that comes with high position. Did you ever think that maybe somebody quite capable was never called to lofty position because that brother or sister could not handle the spotlight? Can the Lord love someone so much that He wants to protect him or her from that attention? Truly, only the Lord can answer this question. But this, to me, is powerful testimony that this Church is indeed run by revelation because this is the Lord's Church. He, and He alone, chooses His leaders at the time He feels they are ready. He will choose them according to His timetable and not ours. It really doesn't matter how well connected a person is, how sharply he or she dresses, how well he or she speaks in public, how well he or she is groomed, or even how well he or she builds connections. *Only* the Lord makes the decision! In the scriptures we read that "[t]he Lord said unto Samuel, Look not on his countenance, or on the height of his stature; because I have refused him: for the Lord seeth not as man seeth; for man looketh on the outward appearance, but the Lord looketh on the heart" (1 Samuel 16:7). Isn't it nice to know that, with God, we don't have to worry about the superficial issues?

Public Praise and Recognition

The witty J. Golden Kimball had this to say about his calling to be a General Authority: "A lot of people in the Church believe that men are called to leadership in the Church by revelation and some do not. But I'll tell you, when the Lord calls an old mule skinner like me to be a General Authority, there's got to be revelation" (Jack M. Lyon, Jay A. Parry and Linda R. Gundry, eds., *Best-Loved Humor of the LDS People*, [Salt Lake City: Deseret Book Co., 1999], 31). Along these same lines, Elder Marvin J. Ashton has said this:

> Be careful, be aware, be wise when people speak well of you. When you are honored, pointed out, and recognized, it can be a cross, especially if you believe what is said about you .... How great, how strong, how pleasing it is to be recognized, honored, and respected, but we must realize in our hearts that true greatness is visiting with the Savior Jesus Christ by helping those who are sick, afflicted, discouraged, homeless, and burdened with crosses. (*Be of Good Cheer* [Salt Lake City: Deseret Book Co., 1987], 38)

Elder Neal A. Maxwell, with his usual flair in the English language, warned against seeking after the "spotlight of adulation" when he said, "When we learn to shine as lights in the world (Philip. 2:15) there is no need to seek to be in the spotlight. Such lesser incandescence is of no interest" (*Men and Women of Christ* [Salt Lake City: Bookcraft, 1991], 28). He's also quoted as saying that "[t]he world's spotlights are not only fleeting, but they employ inferior light!" (Cory H. Maxwell, ed., *The Neal A. Maxwell Quote Book* [Salt Lake City: Bookcraft, 1997], 160).

One way to avoid this "spotlight of adulation" is to literally lose ourselves in performing service for others. This way, we become more concerned about other people's well-being rather than our own. Service to others is the medicine to take if we are feeling a little too much pride or if we need to get our Christlike humility back. Have you ever noticed how addicting service can be? Next time you perform some sort of service to others without the intent of being rewarded, take account of how you feel at that very moment. You'll want to do it again! Some of the best stories come from trying to do service to others without being caught! Delivering a dinner, mowing someone's lawn, washing another's car. The list is endless. These examples are great service projects to do for family home evenings, ones in which everyone can participate, regardless of age.

I had a missionary companion once who made a personal goal to do something for someone else every day of his mission. Late one day, after traveling for some time to get to a particular area, my companion began getting nervous because he had not performed any charitable act that day (in his opinion). While we were driving, he noticed a large box in the middle of the road. He quickly pulled over, snatched the box, broke it down to fit in the car, then drove a little way into town, found a dumpster, and threw the box away. After he had gone through all of this trouble over a box, I asked him why he had done it. He answered, "Just a little bit of service for the day, Elder." That attitude helped my companion to truly be one of the "noble and great ones" written about in Abraham 3:22, which we will discuss further. Remember, when we change what we believe, we literally change what we do, how we act, and who we are.

Complementing this idea, Elder Dallin H. Oaks said this:

Service to others swings our spotlight of priorities outward, away from ourselves. To counter pride we need to give unselfish service. No matter how prominent or praised, the preacher is no better than the hearer, the teacher is no better than the learner. To avoid pride, preachers and teachers and others in prominent positions must struggle not to esteem themselves above their hearers. (*Pure in Heart* [Salt Lake City: Bookcraft, 1988], 143)

It is very dangerous to desire the limelight. As I wrote earlier, we may be kept from certain positions because the Lord, who is the Master of all and knows us so well, may know that for us to have certain callings or positions would be the means of our destruction! President

Howard W. Hunter has this warning for all members of the Church who desire to serve in the more noticeable positions of leadership:

> Beware of the spiritual danger of the spotlight. I think we should be aware that there can be a spiritual danger to those who misunderstand the singularity of always being in the spotlight. They may come to covet the notoriety and thus forget the significance of the service being rendered. You must not allow yourselves to focus on the fleeting light of popularity or substitute that attractive glow for the substance of true, but often anonymous labor that brings the attention of God even if it does not get coverage on the six o'clock news. (*The Teachings of Howard W. Hunter*, ed. Clyde J. Williams [Salt Lake City: Bookcraft, 1997], 66)

How grateful I am to be part of an organization that does not petition for position! Popularity will not get you into the celestial kingdom. Complete compliance to the laws and ordinances of the gospel in conjunction with service to others is the key that unlocks the door.

The Noble and Great Ones

Many members of the Church whom I have spoken to have the mistaken idea that in order to receive a call to lead, they must first have been part of that select group of intelligences whom the prophet Abraham saw when he proclaimed, "Now the Lord had shown unto me, Abraham, the intelligences that were organized before the world was; and among all these there were many of the noble and great ones" (Abraham 3:22). Who were the "noble and great ones" that he saw? How can I become one of them? What did they do that was so special?

It is my belief that *all* members of the Church who are true and faithful to the covenants that they have made to the Lord were and are part of this select group. Certainly, some people have been selected in the pre-earth life to fulfill certain stations while in mortality, but we all have an individual purpose that we need to accomplish. We all have an individual mission to finish. When the Lord said, "These I will make my rulers" (Abraham 3:23), what did He mean by that? Could the Lord have been referring to our next life for some of us? Will we be rulers in the celestial kingdom when we are on the right hand of the Father?

I believe *all of us* who are faithful and diligent in keeping all the commandments that we have been given are part of that great and noble crowd. If we somehow deviate from that intended course, those blessings that would normally have fallen to us would then be given to somebody else. For example:

> Even though we have our free agency here, there are many who were foreordained before the world was, to a greater state than they have prepared themselves for here. *Even though they might have been among the noble and great, from among whom the Father declared he would make his chosen leaders, they may fail of that calling here in mortality.* Then the Lord poses this question: "...and why are they not chosen?" (D&C 121:34). (H. Don Peterson, *The Pearl of Great Price: A History and Commentary* [Salt Lake City: Deseret Book Co., 1987], 280; emphasis added)

There is a great lesson to be learned here, as well, with the following points: "Two answers were given: First, 'Because their hearts are set so much upon the things of this world'.... And second, they '...aspire to the honors of men' (D&C 121:35)." (Ibid., 280).

Clearly, in order to be considered one of the noble and great, we must be able to do certain things. For example, we know that we have to be obedient to the principles of the gospel. "And we will prove them herewith, to see if they will do all things whatsoever the Lord their God shall command them" (Abraham 3:25).

This point is not an option. We must do *all* things. Not some, not most, but *all*. This point is nonnegotiable.

In reference to "[t]hese I will make my rulers" (Abraham 3:23), George Reynolds and Janne M. Sjodahl remarked thus:

> God, the Father of them all, saw that some of His spirit-children were more diligent in serving Him than were others. He perceived that they were good. So standing in their midst, He declared: "These

will I make My rulers." "Abraham," the Lord called him by name, "thou art one of them; thou wast chosen before thou wast born." (*Commentary on the Pearl of Great Price* [Salt Lake City: Deseret Book Co., 1965], 314)

It is my belief that in order to be a noble and great person we need to do noble and great things. What actions imply these qualities? It can be something as simple as spending more time with your children or taking your spouse out on a date. I don't believe that doing something noble and great constitutes an earth-shattering event or a monumental change. I believe that it is those simple acts that many times go unnoticed. Think of some of the teachers you have had in the past. Have they had any influence on you? Are you a better person because of them? I submit to you that the greatest and most noble calling we can have in life is that of a parent. There is nothing more noble or great. The influence you have as a parent easily determines the course of your child's life and ultimate reward.

When we think of past heroes, or key players in mortality, inevitably we always think of Moroni, Helaman, Ruth, Mary Magdalene, Alma the Younger or Peter the Apostle. But even though these great people served in key capacities, is there any question about the faithfulness of some of the less visible players in our scriptures? How about Sam, the brother of Nephi? He is mentioned only a very few times in the Book of Mormon, but his faith is evident. What about Abish, the servant to the queen of the Lamanites? Do you suppose that she was part of that noble and great group spoken of in Abraham chapter three? What about a faithful returned missionary? Certainly, his or her loving commitment of spreading the gospel is a noble and great act.

In the Book of Mormon there is an interesting and powerful verse that says, "Now behold, Helaman and his brethren were *no less serviceable* unto the people than was Moroni; for they did preach the word of God, and they did baptize unto repentance all men whosoever would hearken unto their words" (Alma 48:19; emphasis added).

Many times we forget about those people who serve in quiet faithfulness and whose lives are not in the public spotlight. I submit to you that they are "no less serviceable" than any of the key players found in our scriptures. There are many names of faithful Saints that could be mentioned here who live unnoticed by most, but who, because of their righteousness, are much greater than they know.

I testify to you that we can all be part of that vast group of noble and great ones spoken of in the Pearl of Great Price. The meaning of serviceability to mankind is simply a matter of understanding and perspective. We don't need the spotlight to be able to earn all the blessings promised to us in the scriptures. These blessings are promised us not because we are in the spotlight but because we are actively *doing* the works of righteousness.

CHAPTER FOUR
FASTING

Just after returning home from my seven-month-long deployment to southwest Asia, my family and I were assigned and relocated to a military base on the U.S. east coast. At this time, negotiations for combined military operations were reaching a crescendo about Hungary and Bosnia, and I was terribly afraid that I would get deployed for this operation despite having just returned from a previous deployment. My fears were confirmed one morning when I was called into my commander's office and told of my selection and impending six-month-long deployment. I was devastated. "Not again!" I kept thinking. What would my family think? They had just endured this a few months earlier. This was not the news my wife wanted to hear when I called her on the phone later that morning.

Many thoughts went through my head. And that night when we told the children, the tears started and would not go away. My children kept asking me why the army needed me to go again to another country, since there were so many other soldiers to choose from, and I did not have an adequate answer for them or for my patient wife. That night, as a family, we knelt in very humble prayer and asked our Father in Heaven if there was any way possible for me not to have to go on this deployment and be separated from my family again.

The following Sunday, I had a personal priesthood interview with my elders quorum president, President John Agee. I expressed my fears and concerns to him about my impending deployment and told him how difficult it would be for my family and also for me, having just recently returned from a previous deployment. He suggested that we fast and pray about it. I have to admit that up to that point, fasting had never occurred to me as an option. I enthusiastically accepted his challenge to have a special fast! The date was set. The following Sunday, my wife and I held a fast and, together, asked the Lord to allow me to stay with my family and avoid deployment if at all possible. I am eternally grateful as well to the added faith of President Agee, who joined us in fasting.

My wife and I admitted during our private and companionship prayers that it should not be according to our will but the will of our Father in Heaven. This principle of bending and yielding to what our Father in Heaven wants us to do rather than what we, ourselves, want to do is a difficult one to learn but necessary in order to have our natural dispositions changed. I don't think I ever wanted something so badly in my life. The desire for a change was enormous. I did not want to go on this deployment.

After our mutual fast, countless prayers, and sincere effort to accept the will of the Lord, I went back to work with a better attitude and felt genuinely and significantly closer to my Father in Heaven. I was ready to accept His will, whatever that may be. I began to pack my bags and make plans for the ward to take care of my family. It is a difficult thing to have to leave the welfare of your family in the hands of other people. You just have to trust in the Lord, the bishop, the Relief Society president and the elders quorum president. The home teachers and visiting teachers were also alerted, and they promised to watch out for and care for my little family while I was gone.

A few mornings later, just days before my scheduled departure, I was called into my commander's office once again. I was thinking that they were going to move up my departure date. Instead, I was told that Lieutenant Colonel So-and-So (whom I was supposed to replace in Bosnia) had requested that the position I was to serve in be discontinued and that it no longer needed to be filled. My name was removed from the deployment list! In military circles, this is nothing short of a miracle!

Although I had fasted many times before and have repeated it many times since this experience, I cannot recall when such a miracle has ever occurred in my life. It was the direct result of fasting. I learned for myself the power of a properly held fast. After calling my wife and telling the children, I called my elders quorum president, and he taught me another life lesson. "What did you expect to happen, Brother Greenwood?" President Agee said to me. I guess I had not expected such a miraculous answer to fasting. I thought much about what President Agee had said to me and concluded that I lacked the faith necessary to believe that such a miracle could occur through fasting. Yet I had had enough faith for the miracle to happen. I had always thought that fasting was necessary to change the inner person. I had never really considered that I could use fasting to change something from my environment. I learned a mighty lesson during this experience.

So when is it appropriate to fast? What does it mean to fast? How can fasting help us lose our natural, carnal disposition and help us experience a mighty change? Is there an established structure to fasting? I will address these questions in the following sections.

Why We Fast

Fasting is not something that is new to members of the Church. It is not something new to the world. It has been practiced, followed, and taught for thousands of years. For a principle to have been around as long as fasting has, relatively few people seem to actually know what a fast is and how much it can help them. Even the Savior used the power of the fast to help prepare Himself for His mortal ministry and to assist Him in drawing closer to His Father (see Matthew 4:1–11; Luke 4:1–13).

In my opinion, the best definition for a fast can be found in Isaiah 58:4–7, in which Isaiah reproves the hypocrites and contrasts an artificial fast with a righteous one. Here is the verse:

Behold, ye fast for strife and debate, and to smite with the fist of wickedness: ye shall not fast as ye do this day, to make your voice to be heard on high.

Is it such a fast that I have chosen? a day for a man to afflict his soul? is it to bow down his head as a bulrush, and to spread sackcloth and ashes under him? wilt thou call this a fast, and an acceptable day to the LORD?

Is not this the fast that I have chosen? to loose the bands of wickedness, to undo the heavy burdens, and to let the oppressed go free, and that ye break every yoke?

Is it not to deal thy bread to the hungry, and that thou bring the poor that are cast out to thy house? when thou seest the naked, that thou cover him; and that thou hide not thyself from thine own flesh?

Perhaps the best reasons we fast are personal ones, but here, the prophet Isaiah lists some ideas that are acceptable to the Lord. He tells us fasting can help...

1. **To loose the bands of wickedness.** Fasting can help us overcome bad habits or feelings of unworthiness.
2. **To undo heavy burdens.** Clearly, as discussed earlier, it is a heavy burden to be placed as the shepherd of a flock or to be a leader in the Lord's church. Fasting can help us to become the instrument our Father in Heaven would want us to be.
3. **To let the oppressed go free.** Have you ever fasted during a difficult personal situation or for a suffering friend who needed some additional help? Surely my elders quorum president was doing just that for me.
4. **To break every yoke.** Yokes are problems or hindrances that keep us from our purpose here in life. They are the "fiery darts of the wicked" (Ephesians 6:13–16). We need additional help if we are to succeed in this mission or purpose in life.
5. **To deal thy bread to the hungry and to bring the poor that are cast out to thy house.** This is the great mission of the fast offering—to give of our monetary substance so that others will not have to go hungry or homeless. Fast offerings can also bring people closer to the Savior, who will then lift them to a higher spiritual level.

These are just a few examples of why we may want to fast. Clearly, there are many others. Perhaps you are looking for a better job. Perhaps you want to perform better at the job you have currently. Perhaps there is a point of doctrine on which you need clarification. Maybe you need some help with a wayward child or need to improve your parenting skills. The personal reasons we fast are endless.

Another important issue about fasting to consider is that the Lord does not expect you to fast if you are pregnant, if you are on medication that requires you to eat solids or liquids, or if you have a medical condition that would not make fasting advisable.

A Spiritual Feast

In my opinion, the greatest reason we fast is to draw closer to our Father in Heaven and to ask for special blessings. When we fast, the bond that we have with Him only becomes stronger, as does our faith. We also become more attuned to what we can do to help bless the lives of those around us. Fasting has been and always will be an important principle for us to adopt in our lives. President Howard W. Hunter said this about fasting: "To discipline ourselves through fasting brings us in tune with God, and fast day provides an occasion to set aside the temporal so that we might enjoy the higher qualities of the spiritual. As we fast on that day we learn and better understand the needs of those who are less fortunate" (*The Teachings of Howard W. Hunter,* ed. Clyde J. Williams [Salt Lake City: Bookcraft, 1997], 40). President Gordon B. Hinckley has said: "It is not a burden to refrain from two meals a month and give the value thereof to assist in caring for the poor. It is, rather, a blessing. Not only with physical blessings flow from the observance of this principle, but spiritual values also" (*Teachings of Gordon B. Hinckley,* [Salt Lake City, Utah. Deseret Book Co., 1997], 217-218).

If fasting is done righteously, it is a spiritual feast, because we gain more than we lose. President George Q. Cannon tells us:

It is true that in the book of Doctrine and Covenants the Lord, speaking of the Sabbath and commanding that the food for the day shall "be prepared with singleness of heart," adds, "that thy fasting may be perfect, or, in other words, that thy joy be full. Verily, this is fasting and prayer, or in other words, rejoicing and prayer." (D&C 59:13–14.) But rejoicing in the outpouring of the spirit and feasting upon spiritual things does not imply worldly merry-making …. Humility, contrition, charity—these things constitute rejoicing far beyond anything that the festal board can yield. (*Gospel Truth: Discourses and Writings of President George Q. Cannon,* ed. Jerreld L. Newquist [Salt Lake City: Deseret Book Co., 1987], 404)

Additionally, President Harold B. Lee once said when describing an experience that he had with one of the stakes of the Church in Arizona that after having a day of fasting and prayer, it began to rain. He points out that the Lord had heard the prayers of those Saints. Describing that incident, President Lee said, "If a time comes when things are not going right, and you cannot make a decision in some matter, it is almost always certain evidence that you are not praying enough. Maybe you ought to do a little fasting" (*The Teachings of Harold B. Lee,* ed. Clyde J. Williams [Salt Lake City: Bookcraft, 1996], 124).

Fasting is also what the Apostle James calls practicing "pure religion" (James 1:27). Pure religion is practicing what our Savior taught and doing what we are supposed to do. Such efforts are not going unnoticed. As you do the things our Father in Heaven has requested of you, you will find that He is a generous paymaster, anxious and willing to give us all the things of which we stand in need. What better way of showing our gratitude and appreciation to the Lord than by doing those things He requests of us and by practicing this pure religion? As the Apostle James says in the scriptures, "Pure religion and undefiled before God and the Father is this, To visit the fatherless and widows in their affliction, and to keep himself unspotted from the world" (James 1:27).

What fasting does *not* mean is to go around in sackcloth and ashes, creating ostentatious public displays or outward appearances that announce to the world what it is you are doing. In fact, in my opinion, you shouldn't tell anybody when you're fasting. Even the Savior warned against trying to make our fast visible (see Matthew 6:16–18). We certainly shouldn't "sound a trumpet!" We certainly shouldn't be self-righteous about it. Fasting is a personal and private issue.

Occasionally, there have been times dictated in the past when the Church has informed members to fast for specific reasons. For example, a fast may be held for famine sufferers, as was done for Ethiopia in 1988. Or a bishop may ask that a certain fast be held for one of the families in his ward that needs a special blessing. But for the most part, fasting is a personal issue and should not be advertised, as you would not advertise what is contained in your patriarchal blessing. President George Q. Cannon once wrote:

> It is not enough to bow the head in seeming humility while within there is strife and hardheartedness. We may not understand that even the going without food or the giving of alms to the poor is of itself a passport to divine favor. The idea is that with the outward sign of humility there shall also be the contrition of heart, the charity, the love of fellowman that produce in the worshiper a desire to see and correct his own shortcomings and to strengthen and build up himself as well as his fellowman in faith and excellence. True fasting causes one to put away worldly-mindedness, to feel his weakness as compared with God's might, to draw near to Him in earnest supplication. (*Gospel Truth: Discourses and Writings of President George Q. Cannon,* ed. Jerreld L. Newquist [Salt Lake City: Deseret Book Co., 1987], 404)

As I indicated earlier, the Savior tells us that we need to be discrete about our fasting and that we should not be doing it for public approval. He says in addition, "Moreover when ye fast, be not, as the hypocrites, of a sad countenance: for they disfigure their faces, that they may appear unto men to fast. Verily I say unto you, They have their reward. But thou, when thou fastest, anoint thine head, and wash thy face; That thou appear not unto men to fast, but unto thy Father which is in secret: and thy Father, which seeth in secret, shall reward thee openly" (Matthew 6:16–18).

When we fast, we do it for the Lord and the Lord's influence in our hearts and spirits. Only then will we be fulfilled in purpose and move on to experience the mighty change. We don't need public acceptance, only the approval of our Savior and Redeemer, Jesus Christ, and our Father in Heaven.

Making a Good Fast Great

Fasting is so much more than just going without food for twenty-four hours. Like gifts of the Spirit, the rewards we get may be invisible to the carnal mind, but if we are spiritually in tune, we experience the change of heart and, therefore, lose our disposition to do evil. We begin to want to be with others who have a similar or kindred spirit. It isn't enough just to go through the routine; we need to earnestly strive to help other people and lift them to a higher level. We will experience joy beyond understanding. Joy will happen because we are living a true principle of the gospel. Before I truly understood what a righteous fast was, I just went without food for a time. Essentially, just starving myself. I was going through the routine, not the experience!

I had my first exposure to righteous fasting as a missionary in the Missionary Training Center (MTC) in Provo, Utah. Because I really did not have a testimony of the power of fasting yet, I, along with several other elders, invaded the vending machines. On the evening before fast Sunday, I would wait in line at the vending machines to be able to get some snacks to save and then eat later in the day on fast Sunday. I remember how empty the vending machines were on Monday morning! I wonder if this was a routine procedure or just an isolated incident while I was there. There were also other missionaries whom I recall as very faithful and diligent in the observance of the fast. I imagine they were fasting to be able to be effective missionaries. It was their example to me that gave me the exposure I eventually needed for true, righteous fasting.

The formal observance of a fast day was actually initiated in the early days of the Church by President Brigham Young. It was established that donations for the poor were to be given to the bishop for distribution. We know this from early Church history when President George Q. Cannon wrote the following:

He [President Young] gave instructions that a general fast should be regularly observed throughout Israel and that the food which would have been eaten, or its equivalent, should be given to the poor. The occasion became a time of spiritual refreshing, when in their assemblages the Saints were moved to the exhibition of sincere brotherly love and to the expression of strong testimonies of the truth of the Gospel, accompanied in many instances with powerful manifestations of the spirit and the giving of precious experiences and instructions. (*Gospel Truth: Discourses and Writings of President George Q. Cannon,* ed. Jerreld L. Newquist [Salt Lake City: Deseret Book Co., 1987], 405; brackets in the original)

In my opinion, one of the most neglected Church principles in our hectic-paced world today is that of the fast. There appear to be many members of the Church who simply don't understand the blessings that can come to them for obeying this simple law. Additionally, many members don't seem to understand that it is not a suggestion but a full-fledged commandment. To break this commandment, in my opinion, is not an oversight or a sin of omission but a serious violation of the word of God. The Lord has said to us in the Doctrine and Covenants, "Also, I give unto you a *commandment* that ye shall continue in prayer and *fasting* from this time forth" (D&C 88:76; emphases added). However, I do wish to remind you, as I mentioned earlier, our Father in Heaven will not expect you to fast if you currently have a medical condition which would make fasting inadvisable.

In order to gain all the blessings that are rightfully ours by being obedient to this commandment, we must accompany our fasting with sincere prayer. Fasting is incomplete without it. A person who believes he or she can fast without praying is like one of my children, Conrad, who believes that his formal driving training and education is complete with only a few seconds behind the wheel of a car.

A few years ago, there was a particularly bad winter storm in our area, and I got a call at home late one night from my elders quorum president that he needed some brethren to go to the Church and dig out the walkways from under the snow. I took my boys with me, and we proceeded to do just that. Because of the dark, it was necessary to eventually bring the car up close to where we were digging so that we could use the headlights to aid our vision. We had to move the car a total of about fifteen feet. I asked my oldest son, Conrad, who was only fourteen at the time, to do just that. After verbally coaching him for several minutes on how to nudge the car up a few feet, he enthusiastically left to carry out his assignment. Cautiously, he put the car in drive, took off the emergency brake, and gently coasted the car to where we were standing. Once he got to the right position, I had him stop the car and replace the brake. Conrad got out and, with a grin on his face from ear to ear, said to me, "Dad, I think I have this driving thing down pat!" Well, you can't drive without practice, and you can't fast without prayer.

When we fast, the counsel that leaders of The Church of Jesus Christ of Latter-day Saints have advised is that we skip two meals, which generally occur over a twenty-four hour period. Elder Robert L. Simpson of the Seventy has said on the topic, "In addition to the occasional fasting experience for a special purpose, each member of the Church is expected to miss two meals on the fast and testimony Sunday. To skip two consecutive meals and partake of the third normally constitutes approximately a twenty-four-hour period. Such is the counsel" (*Prayer* [Salt Lake City: Deseret Book Co., 1977], 102). I will discuss the numerous blessings associated with a true fast in later chapters. The process of a devoted fast may not be easy at first, but the Lord will help us if our motives are pure and our desires righteous.

True Fasting

Additionally, Elder Simpson explains three blessings that are associated with fasting. First, he points out that most medical authorities will confirm that our bodies will benefit by an occasional fasting period. It will help to cleanse us. That is a wonderful blessing in itself but certainly not the best reason to fast. Second, he says we should contribute the money saved from missing the meals to help the poor and the needy. He also tells us that we reap enormous spiritual rewards. Remember, these blessings will come to us through our obedience to the commandment of fasting, because they can come in no other way.

The same rules applied to the people from the Book of Mormon some two thousand years ago, as they do to us today. In the Book of Mormon, we read, "Nevertheless they did fast and pray oft, and did wax stronger and stronger in their humility, and firmer and firmer in the faith of Christ, unto the filling their souls with joy and consolation, yea, even to the purifying and the sanctification of their hearts, which sanctification cometh because of their yielding their hearts unto God" (Helaman 3:35). I think we all would like this to happen to us.

Fasting is necessary if we are to perfect our lives. If we are true disciples of the Lord Jesus Christ, we will want to do all things that will enable us to return to live with Him. We will want to associate with others who believe and act like true disciples. Our very natures will improve, and we will begin to experience a change of heart. Elder Simpson continues by saying, "Yes, the law of the fast is a perfect law, and we cannot begin to approach perfection until we decide to make it a part of our lives. When you start and stop the fast is up to you, but wouldn't it be nice to culminate it and be at your spiritual peak for the fast and testimony meeting?" (*Prayer*, 103). I testify that our prayers will take on greater meaning, our testimony will be strengthened, and the windows of heaven will be opened up to us by applying a true fast into our lives. But more importantly, we will be more receptive to the Spirit and know the Lord's will for us.

Preparing in Advance

Fasting is not something that you can attempt to do without preparation, just as an airline pilot would not attempt takeoff without going through an exhaustive preflight checklist. We need to prepare ourselves emotionally, spiritually, and physically before we begin our fast. We need to determine our purpose for fasting and discover where we need divine help. If, for example, your purpose is to seek the Lord's guidance in a decision you have to make, then determine for yourself the best course of action, make the choice, and then fast to see if it is in accordance with what the Savior may want. Talk to your spouse, family member, or a close friend and express your intent to him or her, unless, of course, the reason you're fasting is for a deeply personal issue.

We need to prepare ourselves spiritually by studying the scriptures and other inspirational material, by listening to worthy music, and by attending the temple. We do these things so that we are able to think clearly and feel the Spirit's promptings. We need to be able to have some alone time so that we can effectively communicate with our Father in Heaven and tell Him the issues we have in our hearts. We also need to have a *desire* to know what the Lord would have us do. Then, we need to have the faith to know that an answer *will* come. There is much effort and work involved if we want to have a righteous fast. An answer will not come unless we are willing to put all of the ingredients together. We cannot be effective in our fasting if we are only willing to put forth fifty percent. Rhetoric alone will not do it for us. Neither will simply going through the motions. We must consider our own personal worthiness to determine whether or not we are *able* and *willing* to get an answer to our prayer and fast. We then have to *work* for it. President Harold B. Lee taught this principle when he said the following:

> When we approach the Lord for a blessing we want to make sure that we put ourselves in the state of worthiness to receive that for which we pray. If you want the blessing, don't just kneel down and pray about it. Prepare yourselves in every conceivable way you can in order to make yourselves worthy to receive the blessing you seek. (*The Teachings of Harold B. Lee,* ed. Clyde J. Williams [Salt Lake City: Bookcraft, 1996], 129)

In the Lord's kingdom, actions speak louder than words. Fasting is one way of *showing* our commitment and dedication to our Father in Heaven. He will open the door for us if we knock. He will help us if we ask, but only after much effort and work on our end. We need to take the initial step and demonstrate to Him through fasting that we want His help and assistance. President Howard W. Hunter has said, "There must be desire, effort, and personal preparation. This requires, of course, as you already know, fasting, prayer, searching the scriptures, experience, meditation, and a hungering and thirsting after the righteous life" (*The Teachings of Howard W. Hunter*, ed. Clyde J. Williams [Salt Lake City: Bookcraft, 1997], 36). President Hunter then lists many admonitions from the Lord that can help motivate and prepare us for His help (see D&C 42:61; 18:18; 43:34; 84:85; 90:24). The bottom line is that we simply need to take the time to meditate, ponder, and pray over spiritual matters.

If we fail to apply the key ingredient of prayer to our fasting process, our attempt will fail. We will have just wasted our time. It is also essential and necessary to prepare for fasting by obeying the commandments. We must not leave out any of the ingredients to a righteous fast. To receive an answer, we must show the Lord that He can trust us through our actions; we must show Him that we sincerely desire an answer. Obedience is the best way to demonstrate our love to our Father in Heaven. Then, once we receive an answer to our fast and prayer, whether or not it is the answer we wanted, we must be willing to act upon it (Matthew 7:21). The Lord knows our hearts. He answers our prayers when He knows we are ready to act on what He tells us. Like President Harold B. Lee said, "Your place in the celestial kingdom will be measured by what you do. The Lord's judgment will be according to the deeds of men and women done in the flesh—not by what they profess. It isn't enough just to be good in this church. The all-important thing is that we do good" (*The Teachings of Harold B. Lee*, ed. Clyde J. Williams [Salt Lake City: Bookcraft, 1996], 143).

Part of doing good in the Church is participating in the purifying power of the fast. It keeps us humble and makes us more sensitive to the promptings of the Spirit. By fasting, we are doing what the Lord wants us to do and, more importantly, putting ourselves in a position where the Lord can use us to bless the lives of His other children, whom He loves very much.

There is no shortcut to righteous fasting. You would be deceiving yourself to think that there is such. Everything is sequential and orderly. His house is a house of order, not of confusion (see D&C 132:8). Continuing with his earlier thought about personal preparation, President Howard W. Hunter said, "There can be no spiritual progress and no growth without prayer. The absence of prayer in our work, in our preparation, in our leadership and teaching, is a form of atheism. Prayer and the living of the gospel will give us the spirit of our calling" (*The Teachings of Howard W. Hunter*, ed. Clyde J. Williams [Salt Lake City:

Bookcraft, 1997], 38). Fasting with prayer is the key to changing our natural disposition in this life. It is our answer to progress and growth.

Humility

We must also be humble enough to accept the answer we have been given, or expect to be given, while we fast. Remember, the Lord often inspires others to provide the answers we seek by placing them directly in our path. We must be humble enough to recognize that possibility. President Harold B. Lee once said:

> We must pray with real intent, with desire to know, and with faith on the Lord Jesus Christ; then by the power of the Holy Ghost we may know. That is the only way we can have an answer to prayers .... Each of you, in other words, must stand on your own feet if you will receive the great blessings which the Almighty has in store for you .... Be humble, be prayerful, and the Lord will take you by the hand, as it were, and give you answer to your prayers. (*The Teachings of Harold B. Lee,* ed. Clyde J. Williams [Salt Lake City: Bookcraft, 1996], 126)

True and righteous fasting is not something that can be taken lightly. It requires much work, preparation, and willingness to abide by the principles of the gospel. Fasting is not for the tame of heart. It is for the bold. It is for the fearless. It is for the courageous. It is a principle for the true disciples and followers of Jesus Christ. By being faithful to the principle of fasting, many members of the Church can enjoy blessings that would not normally come to them.

President Harold B. Lee goes on to say that "[i]t isn't the amount of money...that is the important thing; it is the fact that having thus complied with the law, we then qualify ourselves and this church as the kingdom of God. We are then qualified to pray to the Lord, to call and He will answer .... It is this way that the Lord opens the windows of heaven and pours out blessings that we shall hardly be able to receive (see Malachi 3:10)" (*The Teachings of Harold B. Lee,* ed. Clyde J. Williams [Salt Lake City: Bookcraft, 1996], 208).

Once we obey the principles of fasting, slowly, line upon line, we will master ourselves. Our carnal natures will be diminished to make room for a mighty change so that we may fulfill our destiny as part of the great and noble. Only then can the Savior use us to help bless the lives of others in our midst.

CHAPTER FIVE
TRIALS OF FAITH

One of the hardest lessons to learn about life is that in order to make it fulfilling, in order to really make it a first-class experience, we need to have first-class trials. In order to lose our natural disposition toward evil, we need to be active participants in life, ready and willing to accept *all things* that the Lord may have us endure. It is absolutely essential to keep an eternal perspective about trials. Though they are difficult, often painful, and sometimes beyond our understanding, we must remember that these trials will help us in our quest to become more Christlike and help us to endure them better in the future. The pain may not go away, but the perspective will change.

One day at Church, after finishing up with some meetings, I received a note asking my wife and me to go see the bishop before we left for home. Curious, I knocked on his door at the designated time. He warmly received us and, after initiating some light conversation, told me that he had recently received a strong impression that he needed to give me a priesthood blessing. I questioned him about this and told him that everything was fine in our life. I did not think I needed to receive a blessing, but I supported my bishop and told him to proceed. In the blessing, I was told of my Heavenly Father's love for me and that if I ever needed Him, all I had to do was ask. Other inspired promises and blessings were given which I did not fully understand. I left the bishop's office with a sense of gratitude for our inspired leader and even more appreciation for the priesthood but without a complete understanding of why I needed to have this blessing.

A few weeks later, as I was traveling to work very early one October morning, I vocalized a prayer to my Father in Heaven. I remember particularly asking the Lord to help me become more humble. Little did I know of the events that were about to transpire and have such a profound effect on me and my family.

At the time, I was working for a major Fortune 500 company. Things were looking pretty good for me, I thought. I had worked for the establishment for many years and felt my job was secure. After I had already been at work for several hours that day, I was called into the office of one of the senior managers and told that my position was no longer needed and that I was being let go. This caught me totally off guard! I should not have been surprised, and yet I was. For some time, I had been receiving a very subtle impression that I was going to be let go, but in my weakness, I did not recognize it. I kept thinking that it could not happen to me. I learned another of life's hard lessons that day about listening to the promptings of the Holy Ghost.

I was in shock the entire drive home. I was numb and sick with fear for my future. I could not believe that something like this had happened to me. No advance notice, no warning, nothing. It was unfair. I kept thinking to myself, "What about my family? What am I going to do now?" I kept repeating these questions to myself. I had absolutely no idea what I was going to do. I felt like a total failure and as though I had reached rock bottom!

My wife was a tremendous blessing to me at that time. She was very optimistic and really didn't worry much about our misfortune. Her faith was lifting her up, while I was questioning mine. She became stronger, and I became depressed. I felt the experience was completely unfair. Why did I have to endure this? My family and I were living the gospel. We had family prayer and scripture study. We paid our tithes and gave generous fast offerings faithfully. Why would something like this happen to us? What had I done wrong? I could not understand it.

Later that day, I received a phone call from the human resource manager from this company who also happened to be in our ward and was serving in the bishopric at the time. "You're so lucky," he said to me. I was so preoccupied with my thoughts that all I could do was question him. Then my friend told me something that I have never forgotten. He told me that I was lucky because the Lord loved me so much that He wanted to put me through this ordeal to make me a better person. At the time, I didn't really understand what it was he was trying to teach me, but now, in retrospect, I do.

After being completely useless to anybody for about a week, I finally was ready to receive the right insight. I was asleep one night and all of a sudden remembered the priesthood blessing that had been given to me by our faithful bishop. Suddenly, I felt a fresh outlook and felt a reassuring power come over me. I felt my Father's love and humbly got on my knees and asked for His help in securing another livelihood for me that would successfully provide for my family. Almost immediately afterward, my brother called me from Utah and told me of a job opening.

Taken to Our Limits

Although the job only served as a transition until something more permanent opened up, it provided enough money to put food on the table. After accepting the job and moving my family to Utah a few months later, my dream job opened up within the Welfare Department of the Church. I enthusiastically accepted. Had I not been in the Salt Lake valley, I could not have gotten this job with the Church. Things worked out, just not in the way or in the timeframe I had expected them to. But the Lord does not work within our expectations. Looking back on the experience now, I feel I was tried to the very limits of what I was capable of bearing at the time.

Joseph Smith once taught the Quorum of the Twelve as recorded by John Taylor in the *Journal of Discourses*, "You will have all kinds of troubles and trials to pass through. And it is quite as necessary for you to be tried, even as Abraham and other men of God. God will feel after you and he will take hold of you and wrench your very heart strings. And if you cannot stand it, you will not be fit for an inheritance in the Celestial Kingdom of God" ("Scope of the Gospel," *Journal of Discourses*, John Taylor [Salt Lake City, Utah, June 18, 1883], 24:197).

This is one of the most difficult principles to completely understand within the gospel because, in order to understand the growth that can come from trials and tribulations, we have to experience them. Our Father in Heaven uses these experiences to test our faith to see if we will be worthy to stand when all is said and done. Trials put things into an eternal perspective for us and help us become totally reliant upon the graces of our Father in Heaven. Going through such difficulties makes us more like Him because they teach us patience, tolerance, longsuffering, and humility—characteristics of true Christlike discipleship. These attributes are essential for us to become like our Father in Heaven. Trials are not only essential, they are relevant and pertinent to our eternal salvation. Even modern-day scripture affirms the necessity of opposition. An example from such says, "And it must needs be that the devil should tempt the children of men, or they could not be agents unto themselves; for if they never should have bitter they could not know the sweet" (D&C 29:39).

In today's world, especially, I think it takes more effort to remain true and faithful to all the Lord's commandments if we are steadfast and immovable (see Mosiah 5:15) than it does if we are complacent or indifferent. The distractions of today are numerous. Our personal growth and development are sometimes so painstakingly slow that we don't ever think we will get to the point we want to. This is where we learn patience. When we pray for added strength, it won't happen overnight. When we pray for gifts of the Spirit to help us in our callings, they certainly do not happen immediately. When we want to catch the spirit of a calling, such as missionary work, we must offer tremendous effort, desire, and endless prayer. This way, we show our Father in Heaven that we really want the help. The scriptures show us that He will test our endurance and resolve to see if we are *serious* about our commitment to follow Him. Certainly Abraham was being tested when he was asked to sacrifice his son, Isaac. Nephi's faith was tested when he was asked to obtain the brass plates. And when Enos wrestled with the Lord in his prayer, it lasted all day and into the night until he was told that his sins were forgiven (see Enos 1:1–8). There is, and always will be, a certain degree of struggle that accompanies any blessing that we receive from our Father in Heaven. It is through this struggle that our character becomes refined and polished. Our Father in Heaven will test our resolve to see if we will follow through with the righteous desires we have. Glenn Pearson and Reid Bankhead mention this in *Building Faith with the Book of Mormon*:

> Even when our Heavenly Father gives us a commandment, he does not necessarily make it easy for us to comply with it. We sometimes have to surmount great obstacles to fulfill the commandments of the Lord. Joseph Smith's life is a testimony of this fact. Everyone who has struggled with the Lord for an answer to his prayers to the point where he has received the answer knows that it usually does consist of an all-out struggle. (Salt Lake City: Bookcraft, 1986, 33)

We need to make correct and wise decisions and stick to them even when we get ridiculed, ostracized or persecuted for those choices. Integrity is the substance that develops and polishes our character. Gaining spirituality and learning of the knowledge that will eventually save us is a hardship. However, we must do it ourselves. It can't be done for us. It needs to be sought after, struggled and yearned for. But it will come. And when it does, it comes line upon line, precept upon precept. When we get to the Day of Judgment, we will not be able to say, "It's Bill's fault," or "Steve didn't help me." We will be judged on our *own* merits, character and actions, and not somebody else's.

When we ask for a specific blessing, we need to be totally prepared for the ensuing struggle that will come to us. When I prayed for added humility, I lost my job. When we pray for strength to overcome our challenges, it seems that temptation finds the back door. We need to learn to fight in an entirely different way. When we pray as missionaries to be lead to the pure in heart, inevitably we seem to get more persecution and ridicule. We've heard it before that after we show the Lord our resolve and put forth the desired effort on our end, we receive the desired results. And how true it is. As far as our Father in Heaven is concerned, actions really do speak louder than words!

The Blessings of Opposition

Can you imagine a life without opposition? For those who are struggling right now, this idea might sound a little tempting and fantastic. But if you really ponder about it, can you imagine how bleak and empty your life would be? We would all be used to having our own way. We would all be exceptionally lazy because we wouldn't have to work for anything. We would not learn to become masters over ourselves. There would be no growth, no development, no joy in discovering new things, and no victory. I imagine there would be nothing of worth to know, so there would be no reason for a formal school education. Life would be boring, uneventful, and meaningless. Elder Sterling W. Sill explained just how important trials in life are and how much we need them in order to develop when he said, "Has it ever occurred to you that if all of our prayers were answered, no one would ever get sick, no one would ever die; there would be no opposition; we would always get our own way and we would destroy our strength. Oscar Wilde said on one occasion, 'If God wished to punish us, all he would need to do would be to answer our prayers.' I suppose about the worst thing that could ever happen to us would be to have all of our prayers answered. Even our enemies help us by keeping us alert and on our toes" ("Vision" in *BYU Speeches of the Year*, [Provo: Brigham Young University, October 24, 1962], 2).

We understood this principle in our pre-earth life. Prior to our sojourn here on the earth, we elected to follow our Father's plan despite whatever trials or difficulties may come to us. We fully understood what potential problems could happen. We all "shouted for joy" at the opportunities that awaited us (Job 38:7). We also understood that some of us in that earlier council would, because of our agency, make poor choices and would not make it back to the presence of our Father.

President Spencer W. Kimball tells us that *no person* was exempt from understanding the potential trials and tribulations expected during their probation in mortality:

We knew before we were born that we were coming to the earth for bodies and experience and that we would have joys and sorrows, ease and pain, comforts and hardships, health and sickness, successes and disappointments, and we knew also that after a period of life we would die. We accepted all these eventualities with a glad heart, eager to accept both the favorable and unfavorable. Perhaps we were not so much concerned whether we should die of disease, of accident, or of senility. We were willing to take life as it came and as we might organize and control it, and this without murmur, complaint, or unreasonable demands. (*Faith Precedes the Miracle* [Salt Lake City: Deseret Book Co., 1972], 106; emphasis added)

Even though it may seem to some of us that there is no purpose to suffering, we don't understand what the Lord may have for us down the road. Certainly, our trials and tribulations will make us stronger and more developed. But remember, the Lord will always provide inspired leaders to help us through our difficulties. The priesthood is always available, and the Lord will certainly listen and provide comfort as we talk to Him and let Him carry our burdens. We can also be inspired to solve problems ourselves by seeing a scripture with new eyes or catching a detail that we would normally not see. Have you ever noticed how resilient some people are when they are faced with trials or opposition? Could it be that our Father in Heaven is helping them to cope, providing them strength beyond their means, and helping to purify their hearts? We *must* ask for help. We *cannot* do it alone. Despite how strong we may think we are, we need our Father's help.

Categorizing Trials

Understanding and categorizing the purpose of the types of trials we will all have can help us in our determination to eliminate the disposition to do evil and to experience this mighty change of heart for which we so earnestly strive. Elder Neal A. Maxwell profoundly categorizes life's trials into three different categories or types. To summarize his presentation:

1. **Type I** trials are the results of actions we have chosen to do, sins we have consciously made that have repercussions. For example, cheating on a test and being caught and punished.

2. **Type II** trials are simply woven into the fabric of life. An example would be aging and all the trials associated with that.

3. **Type III** trials are the deepest kind of trials, because these trials help to mold us and shape our character. An example of this would be experiencing the loss of a loved one or a crippling disease.

(*All These Things Shall Give Thee Experience* [Salt Lake City: Deseret Book Co., 1979], page 29-30)

Although the first two types certainly develop character, I believe Type III suffering is custom tailored for us personally by a loving Father in Heaven, because He deliberately chooses to school us in order for us to become more like Him. After all, the scriptures tell us, "For whom the Lord loveth he chasteneth, and scourgeth every son whom he receiveth" (Hebrews 12:6). They also say, "Nevertheless the Lord seeth fit to chasten his people; yea, he trieth their patience and their faith" (Mosiah 23:21).

Imagine what kind of person Joseph Smith would have ended up as if he had just decided to get up and walk out of Liberty Jail, state that he had had enough, and turn his back on the experiences that would help to mold him into the type of man he became. Certainly, nobody could find fault with him if he had done these things, but thankfully he submitted to the will of our Father in Heaven. Imagine that the Prophet Abinadi had acquiesced when challenged by the wicked King Noah and his priests, instead of courageously testifying of the truth! Imagine what would have happened if the Savior had walked away from Gethsemane or succumbed to the temptations of the devil while fasting in the wilderness. What if Abraham had decided not to hearken to the voice of the Lord and had, instead, ignored what was asked of him to take Isaac up to Mount Moriah and sacrifice him?

So, with these different types of trials, we can understand the various kinds of schooling that the Lord would have us endure while here in mortality—those that come from the choices that we make, those that come from living, and those that are specifically made for our eternal development. It is impossible to see from the onset the plan that our Father in Heaven has for us. How will He mold us to be the kind of person that He wants us to be? And, more importantly, how will we accept that molding when it comes? Will we humbly accept His will? Or will we complain, whine, gossip, moan, and take the easier path? So many people think that this mortality is the summation of their existence, and, as a result, they make poor choices. Additionally, many people in the Church whom I have met forget that this mortal life is a very small moment in the grand scheme of things. I know that if these good people realized just how much their current method of dealing with trials and tribulations influenced their eternal reward, they would mightily desire a change of heart and work diligently to achieve one. Elder Maxwell explains how important it is to understand this perspective: "No wonder, either, that a long-suffering God does not always punish swiftly. No wonder, either, given the injustice of the human circumstance and the misuse of human moral agency, that we are counseled to endure it well and to view the tribulations through which we pass as being 'but a small moment'" (*But for a Small Moment* [Salt Lake City: Bookcraft, 1986], 116). As I have the opportunity to teach or train others, I try to help them realize this gem and understand the eternal perspective—that each day *does* count and *how* we endure our individual trials and tribulations during our mortal probation has a direct impact on our eternal reward.

Trials in Perspective

We know from the scriptures that a day to the Lord is equal to one thousand years here upon the earth (Abraham 3:4). According to this time measurement, we can truly understand just how short our moment of life is in the grand scheme of things. Let's put this time measurement into even better perspective. If a person lives to the allotted age of man, say eighty-five years, this means that he will have been gone from the presence of our Father in Heaven approximately two hours, one minute, and 30 seconds. A two-year mission, for example, is only 2.85 minutes using the same formula. This would mean that an eight-hour day at work is just a fraction of a second. To make a poor choice, let's say by looking at pornography or cheating on a test for school, would only take a millisecond according to the Lord's timetable. But during that millisecond, we are sending a clear message to our Father in Heaven about where our priorities lie and what is most important to us.

Satan understands this perfectly. He knows how valuable our time is. If Satan can get you to lose your eternal perspective, it will be to his great joy! Do we spend our time doing good to others and loving as the Savior would love, or do we spend our time living on the fringes and being satisfied with complacency? There is so much to lose here in mortality, yet at the same time, there is so much to gain. Once we begin to understand that we *cannot* afford to lose the eternal perspective of things, that life is truly a small moment, then miracles begin to occur in our lives, our hearts begin to change, and we gradually lose that disposition to do evil and instead desire to do good. We need to keep our guard up so that we are not deceived by a change in our perspective.

Elder Sterling W. Sill explained in a 1962 speech that many of us are deceived by this change in our perspective. He said, "That is exactly the thing everyone of us is doing every day because of this deception in perspective which makes everything in the future look unimportant. We trade away God, eternal life and future celestial glory for some present trifle because the things of today seem so important because they are so close by, whereas the more important things are decreased in size because they seem so far away" ("Vision," in BYU *Speeches of the Year,* [Provo: Brigham Young University, 1962], 9).

Trials come to us not because God has forgotten about us or wants to see us struggle but because He wants to bring us closer to Him. Trials help us to rely upon Him. He wants us to return and live with Him forever (see Moses 1:39). But in order to do that, we must endure some of life's curveballs! Deploying and leaving my family in the care of others was a difficult trial for me to endure. How well I remember feeling the Spirit so abundantly while saying my personal prayers during this difficult period of my life. I was being blessed with understanding, strength to endure, and a spirit of peace and calm. Most importantly, I was feeling my Father in Heavens love poured out upon me. He supported me through all the trauma I was feeling. As a result, I became closer to my Heavenly Father. I believe going through that trial also helped prepare me for other trials, like losing my job. Elder Neal A. Maxwell once wrote, "An equally hard but essential doctrine, if we are to understand life itself, is the reality that since this is a gospel of growth and life is a school of experience, God, as a loving Father, will stretch our souls at times .... God will tutor us by trying us because He loves us, not because of indifference! .... This sort of divine design in our lives clearly requires the omniscience of God" (*All These Things Shall Give Thee Experience* [Salt Lake City: Deseret Book Co., 1979], 28).

Additionally, in our modern-day scripture, the Lord says, "And I give unto you a commandment, that ye shall forsake all evil and cleave unto all good, that ye shall live by every word which proceedeth forth out of the mouth of God. For he will give unto the faithful line upon line, precept upon precept; and I will try you and prove you herewith" (D&C 98:11–12).

It is inevitable that we are going to be tried and tested in this life. We can't change that, but we can change how we look at trials and tribulations and how we approach them. Our attitudes, our perspectives, our understandings of the purposes of this life are some of the greatest blessings of true Christlike discipleship. As I have stated earlier, we need to make a cognizant decision to do the things that our Father in Heaven would want us to do. If we are to have these soul-stretching experiences, we must be able to stand up and say we are true followers of the Savior, regardless of the circumstances. Elder Boyd K. Packer has explained it this way:

> I'm not ashamed to say that I want to be good. And I've found in my life that it has been critically important that this was established between me and the Lord so that I knew that He knew which way I had committed my agency. I went before Him and in essence said, "I'm not neutral, and You can do with me what You want. If You need my vote, it's there. I don't care what You do with me, and You don't have to take anything from me because I give it to You—everything, all I own, all I am." And that makes the difference. (*That All May Be Edified* [Salt Lake City: Bookcraft, 1982], 272)

We must remember that amidst all of the opposition we may encounter, through all the trials and tribulations of life, enduring to the end in obedience is the foremost principle we need to adhere to in order to return to live with our Father in Heaven. I was once told that the difference between a champion and a loser is miniscule. It can be just a fraction of an inch. Races, such as automobile races or horse races, used to have special cameras to determine the winner in close finishes. Sometimes these races were so close that it took much magnification and a specialist in the field of photography to determine who won. Imagine how a person must feel to be that close to the prize, that near to winning, and miss it by just a few millimeters! Now imagine how you would feel to have endured almost to the end in your mortal probation, to have almost walked away with the grand prize, only to decide to suddenly quit, yield to temptation, and turn away.

Discovering What Matters

Thankfully, this race to the celestial kingdom is not given to the swift or to the strong in body. It is not given to the temporally successful or the smart. It is not given to the most witty, the most photogenic, the most athletic, the most well stationed, or the most triumphant. Our reward is contingent on enduring to the end by being completely obedient to the commandments of our Father in Heaven and bearing all of the trials and tribulations we may have to endure. President Joseph Fielding Smith said, "The purpose of our mortal existence is that each individual may be tried and tested to see if, through the temptations, trials, and tribulations of mortality, he can maintain a faithful demeanor and prove himself worthy of the exaltation in the kingdom of God. This is the goal we are seeking or should seek, and it is this integrity and perseverance which brings the fullness of life which Lehi has defined as joy" (*Answers to Gospel Questions,* ed. Joseph Fielding Smith, Jr. [Salt Lake City: Deseret Book Co., 1963], 4:73).

It is my prayer that we may truly understand what matters most in life and learn how to approach each of our trials and tribulations. As we show our determination to live all of the commandments that we have been given, our Father in Heaven will bless us accordingly. It is important not only to understand but to *know* that we will not be left on our own. We will be given help when we need it the most. Whatever opposition any of us may be going through at the moment, the Lord is by our side. We may be struggling with the death of a loved one or the loss of a job, or dealing with a wayward child or military deployment. Many of us are struggling financially. Many of us are struggling to find eternal companionship. Whatever our circumstances, the Lord has promised He will never leave. He will always be there for us. He wants to help. He stands at the door waiting for us to answer. All we have to do is ask for help and allow Him into our lives. We need to learn to submit to His will. We need to have the desire. We need to make the choice and then humble ourselves in order to accept whatever our Father in Heaven may want from us. Only then can He help. And, in return, He will hold nothing back once we've submitted. Elder Maxwell agrees:

No matter how serious the trial, how deep the distress, how great the affliction, [God] will never desert us. We have made Him our friend, by obeying His Gospel; and He will stand by us. We may pass through the fiery furnace; we may pass through deep waters; but we shall not be consumed nor overwhelmed. We shall emerge from all these trials and difficulties the better and purer for them, if we only trust in our God and keep His commandments. (*If Thou Endure It Well* [Salt Lake City: Bookcraft, 1996], 21; brackets in original)

Our Father in Heaven knows what's better for us than we do. We know we will have trials and tribulations in this life, but the gospel teaches us the correct priorities and perspectives. Yielding to His will, doing things His way, will only make life better and more meaningful for us.

Let me conclude with an interesting and enlightening teaching from the life of President David O. McKay, which helps us to understand what matters most in this life. Each of us will have a personal interview one day with the Savior Himself, once our probation is over here on earth. Wouldn't it be great to know what He would ask us in advance? By knowing the questions in advance, wouldn't we be able to prepare ourselves better for it? It would almost be like knowing ahead of time what the teacher is going to ask us on the test we are studying for in school! Wouldn't that be nice?

While speaking to employees of the Physical Facilities Department of the Church in June 1965, President David O. McKay taught that the following questions would be asked to each of us when we meet the Savior, and would occur in the following order. This is a summary:

1. The Savior will request an accountability report about your relationship with your wife. Have you actively been engaged in making her happy and ensuring that her needs have been met as an individual?

2. He will want an accountability report about each of your children, individually. He will not attempt to have this for simply a family stewardship but will request information about your relationship to each and every child.

3. He will want to know what you, personally, have done with the talents you were given in the premortal existence.

4. He will want a summary of your activity in your Church assignments. He will not necessarily be interested in what assignments you have had, for in His eyes the home teacher and a mission president are probably equals, but He will request a summary of how you have been of service to your fellow men in your Church assignments.

5. He will have no interest in how you earned your living, but instead, in whether or not you were honest in all your dealings.

6. He will ask for accountability on what you have done to contribute in a positive manner to your community, state, country, and the world.

(Randy L. Bott, *Home with Honor: Helps for Returning Mission   aries* [Salt Lake City: Deseret Book Co., 1995], 169)

Trials and tribulations are painful and no fun to endure, but these experiences will help shape and mold us into the type of people our Father in Heaven wants us to become. We need these challenges in order to achieve our full potential. As difficult as these experiences are, I am grateful for a loving Father who cares so much about me that he wants me to grow. It is my prayer that each of us will be willing and able to endure these hardships as they come to us, and that we will have the understanding that they are for our own good, for a small moment, and for the purpose of helping us to experience the mighty change.

CHAPTER SIX
REPENTANCE

Shortly after I married, I got to know a young man who had recently been excommunicated from the Church. Prior to his excommunication, he had lived a good Christ-centered life. He was a seminary graduate, a returned missionary, and a part of a loving family. He had accomplished much in his life, but he had left it all during a moment of weakness involving a young lady that he had met while serving on his mission. The young woman became interested in missionary discussions, and my friend began helping her to understand the gospel. At the conclusion of his mission, this young lady followed him home. After my friend's release from his mission, he began attending school with ambition and dating this young woman. Shortly afterwards, a moral transgression occurred.

Sometime after his excommunication, I asked my friend if the choices he'd made were worth what they had cost in the loss of his membership in the Church. His answer not only startled me, it frightened me. He said with no hesitation and slight arrogance, "Yes, it was all worth it. I would do it again! I'm not sorry I did it at all!" Although I continued my association with this friend, I seldom saw him after he made that statement. He wanted to have nothing to do with me or with the Church. For the few short moments I did see him, he appeared to be involved in many of the things he had once been counseled never to do. His personal choices took a 180-degree turn from righteousness. He participated in events that are to be shunned and avoided at all costs. He compromised the Word of Wisdom. He ignored the counsel of his parents and his Church leaders. He thought he had discovered true happiness by conforming to the world's view of happiness. He thought he had discovered freedom. I'm sorry to say I do not know what has happened to him since.

As I think back about my friend, this counsel from a wise elder from my mission comes to mind: "The moment may be temporary, but the memory lasts forever." How true this statement is! Unfortunately, some people in this life would choose a few moments of pleasure over eternal life and exaltation. My friend now must live with the choices, memories, and the repercussions of his choices for the rest of his life. With the help of a loving family, a concerned bishop, and devout home teachers, he may see the error of his choices and decide to get his life back in order again and come back into the Church. I pray it will be sooner rather than later. But he will always be welcomed back. However, if he chooses not to come back into the fold, he will have to account for *and* accept responsibility for his wicked choices. My friend has put himself into a position now where he must be very careful because, if he should die before he repents, he will die in his wickedness.

In the Book of Mormon, the Prophet Nephi tells us, "Wherefore, if they should die in their wickedness they must be cast off also, as to the things which are spiritual, which are pertaining to righteousness; wherefore, they must be brought to stand before God, to be judged of their works; and if their works have been filthiness they must needs be filthy; and if they be filthy it must needs be that they cannot dwell in the kingdom of God; if so, the kingdom of God must be filthy also" (1 Nephi 15:33).

This is an understandably frightening concept for some people but a very true principle nonetheless. Repentance is absolutely *essential* if we desire to live again with our Father in Heaven. There is no other course of action. There is not one soul on this planet that is exempt from humbly seeking forgiveness from the Lord, because each of us sin. It doesn't matter who you are. Nobody is exempt. Nobody is perfect. We all need additional help to bring us into the presence of the Lord. President Spencer W. Kimball once wrote that "[w]e might add that one's position makes no difference to the inescapability of the consequences of sin. In the Church, the bishop, the stake president, the apostle—all are subject to the same laws of right living, and penalties follow their sins just as for the other members of the Church. None are exempt from the results of sin, as regards either Church action against the offender or the effects of sin upon the soul" (*The Miracle of Forgiveness* [Salt Lake City: Bookcraft, 1969], 133).

When I was a young adult, another friend of mine whom I knew very well also decided to live a life contrary to the way we believe as members of The Church of Jesus Christ of Latter-day Saints. Most of us in our little group of friends did not agree with the choices this young man made, particularly those of self-indulgence and immorality, but we were careful not to judge him; however, we did let him know that if he ever needed us, we would always be there for him. I once asked this young man why he continued to do what he did, even with the knowledge he had, and, like my friend who had been excommunicated, this man's response also frightened and alarmed me! I can remember it verbatim: "I will repent when I am ready to! In the meantime, I'm having too much fun, and repenting is the last thing in the world that I want to do. Why should I repent now? *I'm not ready to change!*"

My friend's logic was flawed, and his resolve weak, but many people live by this standard. The truth is, though, that it's never too early to repent.

Waiting on Repentance

How do you compassionately respond to such a statement like the one my friend made without offending or sounding self-righteous? I can't recall how I responded at the time, but judging by my friend's actions, I obviously had no impact on his way of life! I often wonder how many lives this person could have touched had he chosen the right path and done the things we are supposed to do. How many souls could he have saved had he gone on a mission? If he eventually has children, how will they view the gospel of Jesus Christ? Will they behave the same way my friend has?

There are *significant* dangers involved if one waits on his or her repentance. In my opinion, the prophet Abinadi from the Book of Mormon addressed the issue best when he said, "But remember that he that persists in his own carnal nature, and goes on in the ways of sin and rebellion against God, remaineth in his fallen state and the devil hath all power over him. Therefore, he is as though there was no redemption made, being an enemy to God; and also is the devil an enemy to God" (Mosiah 16:5).

How would you feel to be categorized as an "enemy to God" and then put into the same grouping as the devil? What a horrible position to be in! We must repent now. We can't afford to wait. Our eternal reward may hang in the balance.

Satan can easily persuade people, particularly the youth, that the principles of the gospel and regulations by which the Church abides are restrictive and limit our ability to attain true happiness. He is very effective in nurturing the perception that living the gospel cannot be fun or rewarding. Then if you do sin, he tells you it's okay. "Don't panic," he says, "because you have all the time in the world to repent!" Enjoy yourself today, because tomorrow you can be sorry. Another tactic Satan uses to keep people from doing good is to give them the impression that if everyone else is doing it, it must be okay. Be careful! Don't fall into this trap! Often, the popular way of doing things in this life is not the right way. These tactics were very prevalent during Book of Mormon times. The Prophet Nephi explained it this way:

> Yea, and there shall be many which shall say: Eat, drink, and be merry, for tomorrow we die; and it shall be well with us.
>
> And there shall also be many which shall say: Eat, drink, and be merry; nevertheless, fear God—he will justify in committing a little sin; yea, lie a little, take the advantage of one because of his words, dig a pit for thy neighbor; there is no harm in this; and do all these things, for tomorrow we die; and if it so be that we are guilty, God will beat us with a few stripes, and at last we shall be saved in the kingdom of God.
>
> Yea, and there shall be many which shall teach after this manner, false and vain and foolish doctrines, and shall be puffed up in their hearts, and shall seek deep to hide their counsels from the Lord; and their works shall be in the dark.

And the blood of the saints shall cry from the ground against them. (2 Nephi 28:7–10)

Practicing true obedience—not because we have to but because we desire the Lord's full blessings—is a big part of overcoming our disposition to do evil and experiencing the mighty change we are working toward. Being faithful and obedient to all the commandments and principles of the gospel is the means of receiving a fullness of joy! As a teacher of the gospel, I have attempted to help the youth and the adults understand this principle. It has been difficult for some to recognize that in order to know the freedom that can come with complete compliance, we must first become compliant! The two thousand stripling warriors understood this doctrine, and as a result, they were protected in times of war. For example, as Helaman explained, "Yea, and they did obey and observe to perform every word of command with *exactness*; yea, and even according to their faith it was done unto them; and I did remember the words which they said unto me that their mothers had taught them" (Alma 57:21; emphasis added).

The gospel is meant to help us, not hinder us. President Ezra Taft Benson explained further:

One of Satan's most frequently used deceptions is the notion that the commandments of God are meant to restrict freedom and limit happiness. This is the first concept I wish to stress: The gospel principles are the steps and guidelines that will help us find true happiness and joy. If we wish to truly repent and come unto Him so that we can be called members of His Church, we must first and foremost come to realize this eternal truth—the gospel plan is the plan of happiness. Violation of the laws of God brings only misery, bondage, and darkness. (*Repentance* [Salt Lake City: Deseret Book Co., 1990], 1)

A key principle to understand is that repentance, in its purest form, is so much more than just a change of behavior. To truly understand repentance it is essential that we understand the Atonement and how the Savior fits into it. Once we begin to have an understanding of the

Atonement, we will begin to appreciate the principle of repentance, discover higher motivation for righteousness and desire to become like He is—perfect in every way. Our self-discipline will be greater than it is now. Repentance will help us. It is the key in our quest to experience the mighty change, to lose our disposition to do evil and instead do good continually.

The Atonement

There is no question that the Atonement is the most important event to have ever transpired on the face of the earth. As I have instructed not only the youth but the adults of the Church, I am amazed to see just how little this event is understood. A true understanding of the Atonement allows us to realize just how much our Father in Heaven loves His children. In the following section, I will address the Atonement and its impact in our lives through four questions.

1. What is the Atonement?

A true understanding of the Atonement is essential to experiencing a mighty change of heart. There are abundant references and excellent materials available to help. We should make every effort possible to read these materials, because without the Atonement we cannot be saved and admitted into our Father's kingdom.

In order to answer this question in its proper perspective, one place that we can turn to is the Doctrine and Covenants, which says these four things about the Atonement: "That he came into the world, even Jesus, to be crucified for the world, and to bear the sins of the world, and to sanctify the world, and to cleanse it from all unrighteousness; That through him all might be saved whom the Father had put into his power and made by him" (D&C 76:41–42).

In the most simple meaning, the Atonement is essentially the act of our Savior bearing the sins of the world for you and me in order to sanctify the world and cleanse it from all unrighteousness. This act alone made it possible for us to return and live with our Father in Heaven with a resurrected body and to become perfect. He enabled us to become clean and pure again, to remember our sins no more (see Isaiah

1:18). The Atonement allows us to be reconciled to our Father in Heaven. In order for this to happen, our Savior needed to endure unimaginable suffering in Gethsemane. This was followed by his voluntary death on the cross. The great selfless sacrifice Jesus Christ made to pay for our sins and overcome spiritual death is called the Atonement. Although all people will be resurrected with a body of flesh and bone, only those who accept the Atonement will be saved from spiritual death. It is a great offense to our Father in Heaven and His Son, Jesus Christ, to think that this subject either bores us or in some way is not applicable to us. Our Savior suffered for everyone. It is the most important event that has ever occurred in the history of mankind!

2. Why is it important to us?

The Atonement is *so* important to us in our lives and to The Church of Jesus Christ of Latter-day Saints that without it we really would not have much as a church. President Howard W. Hunter said once, "If we should eliminate from our religious beliefs the doctrine of the atonement and resurrection of Jesus Christ and the resurrection of mankind, there would be nothing left but a code of ethics. The propositions of ethics may be noble, but they lack those elements of the gospel that lead men to eternal exaltation" (*Conference Report,* April 1969, 138).

3. Why is the Atonement important for us to understand?

The fall of Adam brought two kinds of death into the world. The first death, physical death, is the separation of the spirit from the body. The second kind is spiritual death, the absolute separation from our Father in Heaven (see Alma 12:16; Alma 42:9; Helaman 14:16; D&C 29:41). If these two kinds of death had not been overcome by Jesus' Atonement, two consequences would have occurred. First, our bodies and our spirits would have been separated, never to be able to reunite; and second, we could not live again with our Father in Heaven. However, our wise and loving Father in Heaven prepared a wonderful and merciful plan to save us from physical and spiritual death. He planned for a Savior to come to the earth to redeem us from our sins and from death.

4. How can we apply the principles of the Atonement to our lives and make it part of our character?

How can we make the Atonement part of our lives? We can accept Christ's Atonement by placing our faith and trust in Him. He will not lead us astray. Through this faith, we desire to repent of our sins, we desire to receive baptism and the gift of the Holy Ghost, and we desire to obey His commandments. We must always remember Him. We become faithful disciples of Jesus Christ. In time, our faith grows and gets stronger, and eventually our entire disposition and nature changes until we lose any desire to do evil. In fact, the very thought of doing something wrong will become repulsive to us! We, in turn, are forgiven and cleansed of sin and prepared to return and live forever with our Father in Heaven.

In the Book of Mormon, the people of King Benjamin experienced this change of heart. They were terrified of doing wrong. According to the scriptures, they all cried out with one voice and said, "And we are willing to enter into a covenant with our God to do his will, and to be obedient to his commandments in all things that he shall command us, all the remainder of our days, that we may not bring upon ourselves a never-ending torment, as has been spoken by the angel, that we may not drink out of the cup of the wrath of God" (Mosiah 5:5). Becoming a truly converted individual takes much more effort than Sunday worship. It is a lifetime goal and cannot be achieved overnight. But it will be well worth the effort.

I am so grateful for a loving Savior who endured so much and for descending below all things in order to comprehend all things (see D&C 88:6). It is my prayer that by understanding the Atonement we can come to know on a personal level His love for us.

Remembrance and Repentance:
A Little R & R

A wise friend of mine once said that if you were to take all the words in the English vocabulary and put them in order of importance according to the gospel, the first and most important word would be *remember*. Think about how many times that word is used in the Church.

We use it in the sacrament prayer each week. Taking the sacrament helps us *remember* the covenants we made at baptism. One reason we go back to the temple after taking out our own endowments is to *remember* the covenants we made earlier. We have lessons in Church each week to help us *remember* who we are and where we came from. We have Young Men and Young Women leaders who help the youth of the Church to *remember* to do the things they are supposed to do. We serve missions to bring people to a *remembrance* of where they came from and why they are here and where they are going. We honor people by dedicating buildings, like the ones at BYU, in that person's name to help us *remember* them and their accomplishments. A quick computer search through our scriptures shows that the word *remember* is used 554 times! Remembrance is a large part of our faith.

We must always remember the sacrifice that our Savior made for us. One of the greatest traps we can fall into in this life is thinking that the Atonement is not applicable to us and that it is really no big deal. It *is* a big deal. Turning your back on the Savior is the greatest offense you can show Him. You can't just say "Big deal" or "So what?" or "I don't care." If someone saves us from an impending death, for example, how do we honor them? We *remember* them. One of the greatest people I ever knew was killed while serving a mission for the Church. I honored his memory by naming my first son after him. I can't help but think of this young man every time I call out my son's name.

An understanding of the Atonement will help us on our pathway toward perfection and allow us to change our dispositions and carnal nature. When President Marion G. Romney would take the sacrament each week, he would say to himself as the bread and water came to his lips, "I do remember thee" ("Reverence," *Ensign*, October 1976, 2–3).

Similarly, President Howard W. Hunter once said this, speaking directly to the youth of the Church:

A study of the life of Christ and a testimony of his reality is something each of us should seek. As we come to understand his mission, and the atonement which he wrought, we will desire to live more like him. We especially encourage the young men and young women to come to know the reason for the atoning sacrifice of our

Lord. When temptations come, as they surely will, an understanding of the Savior's agony in Gethsemane and his eventual death on the cross will be a reminder to you to avoid any activity that would cause the Savior more pain. (*The Teachings of Howard W. Hunter,* ed. Clyde J. Williams [Salt Lake City: Bookcraft, 1997], 31)

I often think of the people who have had the biggest influence in my life. There is something about them that I want to emulate in my own life. Many traits such as spirituality, humility, humor or willingness to serve are great qualities to emulate in our lives. We watch these people, study them, and we want to be like them. Likewise, each of us should study the life of Christ and seek a testimony of His reality. As President Hunter indicated, when we come to understand His mission and the Atonement, which He wrought for us voluntarily, we will desire to become more like Him. It is inevitable. When temptation comes, *remember* the Atonement. An understanding of the Savior's agony in Gethsemane and His eventual death upon the cross will be a reminder to us to avoid any activities that would cause the Savior more pain. We must personalize the Atonement. Christ died for *us*.

If your sins or something else in your life are keeping you from complete compliance to the gospel, repent and do all that you can to get back onto that straight and narrow path. Talk to your bishop, and he will tell you what to do to help you get back into full activity again and to have a clean slate. Many people today are afraid to take that initial step. You are never alone. I imagine that if the veil were taken from your eyes, you would see Mormon, Moroni, Nephi, Helaman and his stripling warriors, and others all standing beside you. How can you do wrong with people like this cheering for you? Even the Savior Himself will stand beside you in your moment of decision. The Lord has said, "Come now, and let us reason together, saith the LORD: though your sins be as scarlet, they shall be as white as snow; though they be red like crimson, they shall be as wool" (Isaiah 1:18).

As I indicated at the beginning of this chapter, I have met many people in my life who have said to me that they are not yet ready to stop what they are doing and repent and seek forgiveness from the Lord. They are under the false impression that they can party it up now and still be able to do all those things in the Church which are necessary to live again with our Father in Heaven. This path is a very dangerous one for two reasons. First, the individuals who follow it will want to do more and more sin until it becomes very easy for them to do. Like the funnel effect we discussed in chapter two, sinning can become much like a death dive, spiraling out of control. Second, it is likely they may never come back into the fold, thereby forfeiting their inheritance in the celestial kingdom.

At a youth event once, I told a young lady about this doctrine of putting off her repentance, and she laughed at me and advised me that my thinking was old-fashioned. After a while, the same young lady became a teenage mother, dropped out of high school, and eventually left the Church entirely. I do not know what has happened to her since.

Sometimes those in authority must speak very plainly and directly about the principles of the gospel in order to make them understood. It may be necessary at times to show tough love as Enos tells us to do in the Book of Mormon when he says, "And there was nothing save it was exceeding harshness, preaching and prophesying of wars, and contentions, and destructions, and continually reminding them of death, and the duration of eternity, and the judgments and the power of God, and all these things—stirring them up continually to keep them in the fear of the Lord. I say there was nothing short of these things, and exceedingly great plainness of speech, would keep them from going down speedily to destruction" (Enos 1:23).

We must be able to accept and understand the Atonement and have it come into our lives if we are to return and live with our Father in Heaven. There is no other way. Imagine how a loving father must feel to see poor choices being made by his children and to see his own children consciously turn their backs on everything good and noble and refuse to return to his presence. How do you think this loving father would feel? The time will come when these children of our Father in Heaven who have chosen to follow after wickedness, despite all our efforts to get them to come back into the fold, must fully account for their wicked actions. Thankfully, some *will* come back and find that our Savior was, and always has been, there waiting for them with open arms. Others will still not come back, despite all our best efforts. At that time, there truly will be weeping and wailing when the wicked realize what it is they have so willingly sacrificed.

The prophet Alma was understandably worried about his son Corianton when he told him the following: "And then shall it come to pass, that the spirits of the wicked, yea, who are evil—for behold, they have no part nor portion of the Spirit of the Lord; for behold, they chose evil works rather than good; therefore the spirit of the devil did enter into them, and take possession of their house—and these shall be cast out into outer darkness; there shall be weeping, and wailing, and gnashing of teeth, and this because of their own iniquity, being led captive by the will of the devil" (Alma 40:13). It is my greatest prayer that we can all understand the importance of the Atonement and how it can change our lives and motivate us to be better people. I know that as we study the life of the Savior, we will desire to be more like Him, and by becoming more like Him, we will have a change of heart. The Atonement is truly the greatest event that has ever occurred for us. It will help us to put the things of this world into an eternal perspective, helping us to know what matters most. Working alongside the Atonement is the blessing and gift of prayer.

Prayer

Prayer is the key to seeking repentance. Some people say that they can't pray or they don't feel worthy enough to pray. This is a lie originated from the master of lies: Satan. He does not want you to pray to your Father in Heaven. He wants to use you as a tool to further *his* work. He knows that misery loves company and he will do all he can to make you feel comfortable in your sins. Satan knows that if he can get you to fall, you may be able to bring others down with you. But if we desire to come back into the fold, it is absolutely essential to pray.

Bishop H. Burke Peterson has offered some very profound advice on praying. His directions have inspired me through the years. They are as follows:

As you feel the need to confide in the Lord or to improve the quality of your visits with him—to pray, if you please—may I suggest a process to follow: go where you can be alone, where you can think, where you can kneel, where you can speak out loud to him. Think to whom you are speaking. Address him as your Father and your friend. Now tell him things you really feel to tell him—not trite phrases that have little meaning, but have a sincere, heartfelt conversation with him. (*Prayer* [Salt Lake City: Deseret Book Co., 1977], 108)

Prayer takes a lot of concentration. As Bishop Peterson tells us, we should go someplace where we can be alone. Even using a bathroom or closet will do. Visualizing our Father in Heaven in our mind's eye can be very helpful because it is to Him that we are speaking. We need to confide in Him and ask Him for forgiveness. Then, we need to be willing to listen to His answers. Listening is also a very essential part of praying. He will answer us, but His answers come ever so quietly. We must be willing to listen with all of our hearts or we will never recognize the answers when they come. Bishop Peterson tells us that most answers from the Lord are felt in our hearts as a warm, comfortable expression, or they may come as thoughts to our mind. Regardless, these answers will come to only those who are prepared to receive them and are willing to listen.

Repentance is fundamental in our spiritual development. The Savior has commanded us to constantly seek repentance. If we are to be true disciples of the Master, we cannot afford to neglect this principle. The Lord has told us, "Say nothing but repentance unto this generation; keep my commandments, and assist to bring forth my work, according to my commandments, and you shall be blessed" (D&C 6:9).

Repentance and remembrance motivate me to become a better person. How grateful I am for a kind, loving Father in Heaven who provided a means for me to be able to return to live with Him. Through the Savior, we can overcome all of our bad habits, change our hearts, and become pure again.

CHAPTER SEVEN
GOSSIPING AND BACKBITING

My family and I have had the fortune of having lived in many wards and stakes around the country and overseas. These have been wonderful experiences for us as we have gotten to know many people from many different backgrounds. We have always been able to find wards that have welcomed us with open arms. The Church is truly an international church with members who are "anxiously engaged in a good cause" (D&C 58:27). However, I found it interesting how some members of the Church here and overseas would come to us, once we had moved into the new ward, and immediately start telling us about Sister So-and-So or Brother You-Know-Who and let us know about how things should be run or what a particular person could be doing better in the ward. It is almost as if they felt compelled to tell us the real truth (according to them) about the ward we had just moved into. We've heard this kind of gossip from the old and wrinkled and the newly married around the world. It's almost as if it were human nature to indulge in these sins.

In my opinion, gossiping and backbiting, these two evil twins, are some of the hardest abominations to let go of. They can and do hold us back from progressing and overcoming our disposition to do evil. Unfortunately, it seems that everyone has, at one time or another, gossiped or had something negative to say about somebody. But what exactly are gossiping and backbiting? How can we avoid them? How can we change our thinking to rid ourselves of these atrocities?

According to Webster's 1828 Dictionary, *gossiping* means "to run about and tattle; to tell idle tales." In the same dictionary, *backbiting* is defined as "the act of slandering the absent; secret calumny." Slandering is the act of defaming people, saying bad things about them when they aren't around to hear it or defend themselves. Calumny is the act of knowingly or maliciously making conversation with the intent to injure another. These definitions have been around since the early nineteenth century, and the practices, much longer. And look how true they still are today. Time changes many things, but apparently not human nature. Think of a person who gossips; doesn't that person essentially run around and tell idle tales about others? Does he or she appear to take pride in their supposed knowledge about others? Of course they do.

We know that the Lord would look down on these practices. Let's see what the Brethren have to say about it. Elder Bruce R. McConkie, in his book *Mormon Doctrine* said, "Gossip ordinarily consists in talebearing, in spreading scandal, in engaging in familiar or idle conversation dealing personally with other people's affairs. Frequently the reports are false; almost always they are so exaggerated and twisted as to give an unfair perspective; and in nearly every case they redound to the discredit of the persons under consideration. It follows that gossip is unwholesome, serves no beneficial purpose, and should be shunned" (2nd ed. [Salt Lake City: Bookcraft, 1966], 336). In the same book, Elder McConkie describes backbiting: "To backbite is to slander one who is not present. It is a wicked, evil practice, hated of God and fostered by Satan. (Ps. 15:3; Rom. 1:30; 2 Cor. 12:20.) It is the express appointment of the teachers in the Aaronic Priesthood—as part of their mission to do home teaching—to see that there is no backbiting in the Church (D&C 20:54)" (Ibid., 69). If we really desire to have "a pure heart and clean hands" (Alma 5:19) and go from good to better, it is important for us to understand the seriousness and also the repercussions of these evil twin behaviors. Fortunately for us, there is much written on the subject in the scriptures and spoken by our Church leaders.

The Consequences of Gossiping and Backbiting

The Lord has been very direct and specific with regard to gossiping and backbiting. He uses very plain language that is easy to understand. The action of gossiping and its subsequent consequences have been clearly referred to in the scriptures. For example: "Let no corrupt communication proceed out of your mouth, but that which is good to the use of edifying, that it may minister grace unto the hearers. And grieve not the holy Spirit of God, whereby ye are sealed unto the day of redemption. Let all bitterness, and wrath, and anger, and clamour, and evil speaking, be put away from you, with all malice" (Ephesians 4:29–31).

Any kind of "evil speaking" is not in harmony with Christ's teachings. There is a good feeling that comes to you when you pay a person a compliment or say good things about someone. You are lifting that person. You are bringing him or her up to a higher level, emotionally and spiritually.

As a parent, I love to hear when my children compliment each other. Learning to praise one another helps them to grow together as a family unit. I believe the same growth occurs when we express our gratitude and appreciation to others outside of our nuclear family. In the scriptures we read that we should "cease to contend one with another; cease to speak evil one of another. Cease drunkenness; and let your words tend to edifying one another" (D&C 136:23–24). In this specific example, the Lord is being very direct. Clearly, He wants us to speak only well of each other. It is something that we need to do all of the time. Not part or most or even some of the time, but *all* of the time!

I find it intriguing that the Lord details specifically that one of the functions or duties of our young priesthood holders is to ensure that there is no backbiting or evil speaking. For example, He says, "The teacher's duty is to watch over the church always, and be with and strengthen them; And see that there is no iniquity in the church, neither hardness with each other, neither lying, backbiting, nor evil speaking" (D&C 20:53–54). Since we all know that we need to be as "little children" (3 Nephi 9:22) in order to enter the kingdom of God, we know that we need to follow this example. Also, the Book of Mormon adds the following:

> And I would that ye should remember, that whosoever among you borroweth of his neighbor should return the thing that he borroweth, according as he doth agree, or else thou shalt commit sin; and perhaps thou shalt cause thy neighbor to commit sin also.
>
> And finally, I cannot tell you all the things whereby ye may commit sin; for there are divers ways and means, even so many that I cannot number them.
>
> But this much I can tell you, that if ye do not watch yourselves, and your thoughts, and your words, and your deeds, and observe the commandments of God, and continue in the faith of what ye have heard concerning the coming of our Lord, even unto the end of your lives, ye must perish. And now, O man, remember, and perish not. (Mosiah 4:28–30)

The Lord knows that gossiping and backbiting are rooted in lies and half-truths. He takes lying very seriously and has some strong words to say about people who lie: "Wo unto the liar, for he shall be thrust down to hell" (2 Nephi 9:34). Incidentally, as a parent, I use this particular verse of scripture many times for my children's benefit…and for my benefit, too!

As we go through life, we sometimes hear things about ourselves, inadvertently, from other sources, that we wish we hadn't heard! We may hear these things secondhand or we may chance upon someone or a group of people who may be saying untruths and rumors about us that we were not intended to hear. This is particularly true in the schools for our young people. How many days have been ruined when we were younger, and how many times have our delicate egos hurt because we heard a bit of gossip about ourselves that was not true or had been exaggerated? How many mean-spirited people just wanted to spread false rumors about you? Our own tongues can often be very mean and hostile weapons as James 3:8 so clearly states: "But the tongue can no man tame; it is an unruly evil, full of deadly poison." Very true words, indeed!

Elder Milton R. Hunter of the First Quorum of the Seventy has this to say about gossiping and backbiting:

> It seems that ofttimes we get a certain degree of satisfaction or even joy out of saying bad things about other people .... Sometimes I gossip and judge others, and when I do it I act unrighteously before the Lord. My heart tells me I would like to repent, I would like to overcome my weakness of gossiping and saying bad things about other people. I am sure that you feel the same as I do. (*Conference Report,* October 1960, 24)

Many presidents of the Church have been very candid in their speaking out against gossiping and backbiting. For example, President David O. McKay advised us to "avoid evil speaking...slander and gossip," saying, "These are poisons to the soul to those who indulge. Evil speaking injures the reviler more than the reviled" (*Conference Report,* April 1953, 59–60).

Also, President Harold B. Lee has instructed us that the single most important commandment for us to follow today is the one with which we are struggling the most. For example, if gossiping or backstabbing is our biggest challenge, then it should be the most important commandment for us. Specifically, President Lee has said the following:

> Turn from the thing that you have been doing that is wrong. The most important of all the commandments of God is that one that you are having the most difficulty keeping today. If it is one of dishonesty, if it is one of unchastity, if it is one of falsifying, not telling the truth, today is the day for you to work on that until you have been able to conquer that weakness. Put that aright and then you start on the next one that is most difficult for you to keep. (*The Teachings of Harold B. Lee,* ed. Clyde J. Williams [Salt Lake City: Bookcraft, 1996], 82)

Additionally, President George Albert Smith said that much pain and suffering in the world are the direct result of others gossiping and backstabbing. President Smith also said that a gossip is never truly happy and that he or she is in Satan's company when they are gossiping about their brothers and sisters. To quote President Smith:

> Think of the sorrow and distress in the world, as a result of men and women gossiping about their neighbors, testifying to things, or referring to things that are not true, and implying that they are true .... This is one of the transgressions that the Lord points out particularly, and we ought to be very careful. We should never testify to anything that is untrue. And if we are truthful always, our Heavenly Father has assured us happiness. (*Conference Report*, April 1944, 29)

What it all comes down to is how well we are able to control our thoughts. Each of us needs to be able to serve the Lord with his or her entire mind in order to be effective in overcoming that natural disposition to do evil. Being able to control our thoughts and minds is one of the ultimate levels of dedication. If we can control our thoughts, we will not fall victim to this powerful abomination of gossiping and backbiting. Eventually, others will see that we desire not to allow these abominations into our lives. Imagine the effect this will have on our surroundings. Imagine how many lives will be blessed by our example and how many people will come back into the fold. How many members of the Church have been hurt unnecessarily by overhearing something that was being said about them?

A few years ago, a family got baptized into our ward and began enthusiastically to do all the things necessary to get sealed in the temple. Once they were baptized, home teachers and visiting teachers were assigned. From a fellowship perspective, everything appeared to be working. Friends were made, callings were issued, and the priesthood was given to the husband. This family was well on their way to becoming an eternal family.

One particular Sunday at Church, the family overheard a negative comment about the clothing that some of them wore. This new family that so many people had helped to bring into the kingdom and that was so close to marrying in the temple became greatly offended and chose to stop coming to Church. I'm sad to say this is nothing new. How many people have stopped coming to Church because of gossip? In my opinion, this was entirely preventable. The ward made an effort to get this fine family back into the fold. Nothing we could do would bring these people back to Church. They had been hurt very deeply.

Consistently controlling our conversations is closely related to controlling our thoughts. When we succeed at fully serving the Lord with our minds, we will want to serve others and do all that we can to further the work of the Lord here upon the earth.

There are several references throughout the scriptures telling us to serve the Lord with all of our heart, might, *mind* and strength (see D&C 4:2; D&C 59:5). By applying these qualities, we will then qualify for a full endowment of the Spirit. However, as I have expressed many times, the Lord cares much more about our actions than our words. In the Doctrine and Covenants we read this: "Let thy bowels also be full of charity toward all men, and to the household of faith, and let virtue garnish thy thoughts unceasingly; then shall thy confidence wax strong in the presence of God; and the doctrine of the priesthood shall distil upon thy soul as the dews from heaven" (D&C 121:45). Through learning how to focus our thoughts and through serving the Lord with not just our heart, might, and strength, but also our mind, we will be in a position to be able to hasten a mighty change within ourselves and be used as an instrument to further His work on the earth.

Focusing Our Thoughts

Unfortunately, many people make very little effort to discipline their thoughts. They may exercise some effort to avoid vulgar and obscene ones, but the Lord expects each of us to cast away *all* our idle thoughts (see D&C 88:69). This means that if our thoughts are not productive, edifying, or filled with virtue, then we have the added responsibility *and* expectation of replacing them with productive or edifying thoughts if we are serious about changing our natures. It will significantly help us to keep our thoughts filled with virtue unceasingly if we remember that our Father in Heaven knows all of our thoughts. He tells us in the scriptures "that thou mayest know that there is *none else* save God that knowest thy thoughts and the intents of thy heart" (D&C 6:16; emphasis added).

We can obtain this level of dedication and learn to shun gossiping and backbiting by striving consistently over a sustained period of time to obtain it. We will have to make an extremely strong effort, initially, to achieve the level of dedication the Lord expects of us, but we can do it. We will be tested to the very core in order for us to prove our dedication. We must do it if we are serious in our desire to serve Him to the end and return back to our Father in Heaven. Learning to shun gossiping and backbiting will be difficult at first, but you will find that as you exert some effort, the Lord will bless you abundantly. You will soon discover that a high level of dedication, once established, is much easier to maintain. When we apply ourselves and make the effort, the Lord will help us to control our thoughts, and we will be able to enjoy the full companionship of the Holy Ghost. We will shun the very thought of gossiping and backbiting. If we dedicate ourselves, we will not be juvenile, immature, or light-minded. Or at least we will be aware of it when we are and will be able to make a change. But, more importantly, we will not be as vulnerable to the enticing of Satan, especially when it comes to these two sins.

But what does it take to control our thoughts so that we don't continue to harbor bad thoughts about people or to talk about them behind their backs? I believe that mental exertion involves the following basic steps:

1. **Train yourself to be conscious of your thoughts**, particularly when you feel compelled to talk about others in a negative light or in a way that makes you appear to be better than them. We are all brothers and sisters. Nobody is better than anybody else, despite our calling, financial status, education level or network of friends. We all have different strengths and weaknesses, but we all have the same noble posterity with the same divine potential.

2. **Learn to scrutinize your thoughts to determine if they add to or detract from your faith**. Simply put, are your thoughts

filled with light or darkness? Do your thoughts edify and lift up or tear down and demean? Try to think of only the good in people. All people have good in them, we just need to find it.

3. **If a thought detracts from your faith, replace it with a thought that is based on faith.** Fill your mind with light, such as a Church song or a scripture. Bear to yourself your testimony. Think of your own baptism, temple marriage, prior missionary experience. You can even focus on a wonderful sacrament meeting talk. There are many examples that can be used.

To exercise mental exertion effectively, you must have power and dominion over your mind. It is very similar to dieting. Learning to control our appetites is, at times, difficult to do, particularly when those around us are eating some of our favorite meals! You cannot allow your mind to be easily distracted or to focus on something that is extraneous to your desired blessing. For instance, when you call upon the Lord for His blessings, do you find various thoughts popping into your mind regarding trivial matters or other mundane preoccupations? The next time you pray or meditate, see if you have the ability to keep your mind from wandering. It will be difficult at first, but eventually, you will find that these moments with our Father in Heaven are very personal, sacred, and extremely rewarding.

As you may expect, you will find that as you attempt to control your thoughts and cease from gossiping and backbiting, the devil will bring things to your view to divert you from your noble objective. Opportunities may present themselves where it will be very difficult *not* to gossip or backbite. You may even hear of things that you want to share with others that would be inappropriate. But despite the temptation to join in, exercise your faith to the point that your eye will be single to His glory, and you will be able to unlock the powers of heaven by your faith. President Brigham Young once said, "The greatest mystery a man ever learned, is to know how to control the human mind, and bring every faculty and power of the same in subjection to Jesus Christ; this is the greatest mystery we have to learn while in these tabernacles of clay" ("Self-Government—Mysteries—Recreation and

Amusement, Not in Themselves Sinful" *Journal of Discourses,* Brigham Young, [Salt Lake City, Utah, April 9, 1852], 1:47).

In a very literal sense, desired ends must be created spiritually in the mind before they can be realized. Envision yourself as one who does not indulge in gossip or backbiting or whatever bad habit you may have at the moment. Once you see yourself in this light, you're one step closer to making it a reality. Visualizing what we can accomplish with the Lord's help is a form of vision. Seeing things in your mind's eye is an example of seeing with an "eye of faith," as the prophet Alma the Younger taught (see Alma 5:15). With the Lord's help, we can overcome and triumph over all our bad habits, including gossiping and backbiting. Ridding ourselves of these twin evils is essential for us to lose our desire to do evil and only desire to do good continually, and to begin to experience a mighty change, the process of going from good to better.

To fully experience the mighty change, we should apply what President David O. McKay once said and realize that gossiping, backbiting and faultfinding are "weeds of discord and thrive best in *superficial* minds, as fungus grows best on weakened plants. 'Bear ye one another's burdens,' but do not add to these burdens by gossiping about your neighbors or by spreading slander" (*Pathways to Happiness,* ed. Llewelyn R. McKay [Salt Lake City: Bookcraft, Inc., 1957], 210; emphasis added). We are all born with the tendency toward a superficial mind. What we need to do as we grow is overcome that. Conquering our superficial nature is also necessary if we are going to eliminate the practices of gossiping and backbiting from our lives and experience the mighty change.

How grateful I am for my association with people who are wise enough to give me council when I veer off the path I intend to go on and who have taught me to get the facts right before any judgment is made.

CHAPTER EIGHT
SERVICE

One night after I had finished the initial draft of this book, I couldn't sleep. I couldn't shake the feeling that something was missing from the manuscript. I kept pondering over this thought until it occurred to me that I was missing a key ingredient that is imperative in helping change our disposition so that we want to do good—something essential to experiencing a true change of heart. Service.

Initially, I was confused about how I could have missed such a key ingredient. Imagine how bland our lives would be without service to others. Imagine the life of our Savior if He had not served others. We can feel His love for us because He wants to serve us and help us to succeed. We learn to love others through service. It has always been that way, and it will always be that way. Most missionaries have a hard time leaving their areas for a transfer or leaving the mission field at the conclusion of their missions because they have learned to love the people and their companions so deeply through various acts of service. Service is an essential part of changing our hearts and minds in order to have no more disposition to do evil. Service teaches us to love others and forget about our own troubles.

Some of my fondest memories of service are from when I was a young deacon in the Aaronic Priesthood. My father took me, from time to time, to do service at the Church farm, which was located about forty miles from our house. On my very first trip to the Church farm, I didn't have a clue what to expect. I envisioned pulling weeds or cleaning the animal stalls. To be quite candid, I was a little irritated that Dad would ask me to give up my Saturday to do something at the Church farm. I wanted to sleep in! I was going through my macho identity stage (I thought I was the great and powerful Oz!), so I knew I had to do something on the farm that would showcase me and my wonderful talents by being very physical and praiseworthy in order to have my ego satisfied. When we arrived at the farm, we discovered that our assignment was to pluck the peaches from the trees and put them into boxes for canning. Various chores related to that were assigned to some of the men, and finally, after what felt like an eternity, to me. The man in charge asked me what I wanted to do. My ego was bruised! Ideally, he should have asked me first! Unfortunately, I felt like the last kid left standing when the teams are made up in elementary school! Puffing out my chest, I enthusiastically told him to give me the hardest job available. "I can do it all!" was my less-than-humble response.

With a smile on his face, he brought me over to the tractor and told me to gather up all the boxes of peaches that the members would pluck from the trees and stack them on his trailer. After the trailer was full, we would then unpack them at the cannery and go back to the orchard for more peaches. This process was repeated several times. I recall how sore my muscles were the next morning from all the lifting I had done, but, more importantly, I also remember to this day the feeling of joy I experienced and the genuine desire to *want* to do service again. As I grew older, these feelings would manifest themselves again each time some act of service was rendered to others, particularly when I served my mission in Australia and prayed to be able to do some sort of service each day.

I once heard an old fable that taught me a significant lesson about how service can be nurtured. The fable says that one night a young man had a dream. He dreamed there was a new store in a nearby shopping mall. He went in and saw an angel behind a counter. Nervously, he asked what the shop sold. "Everything your heart desires," replied the angel. "Then I want peace on earth," said the idealist. "I want an end to famine, sorrow, and disease." "Just a moment," replied the angel. "You haven't understood. We don't sell fruit here—only seeds." These "seeds" of service grow and develop with time and help us in our desire to serve others. But, in order to grow, we need to care for them and do whatever we can to help them grow.

Most of us are familiar with various scriptures which discuss service to some degree or another, such as the lesson taught to us by King Benjamin in the Book of Mormon, which says, "And behold, I tell you these things that ye may learn wisdom; that ye may learn that when ye are in the service of your fellow beings ye are only in the service of your God" (Mosiah 2:17). The Doctrine and Covenants also adds to this: "Therefore, O ye that embark in the service of God, see that ye serve him with all your heart, might, mind and strength, that ye may stand blameless before God at the last day" (D&C 4:2). I believe that these verses apply to anybody who serves the Lord in whatever capacity. We are all embarked in the service of God, regardless of our calling.

The Message for Our Time

Service is a topic that has been addressed on many occasions by the Brethren. Clearly, it is one of the most important messages for our time. President Ezra Taft Benson made this statement regarding service:

> The Lord has a way of blessing His children, magnifying them, and bringing them joy and happiness wherever they serve in His kingdom so long as they serve Him with all their heart, might, mind, and strength .... If you would find yourself, learn to deny yourself for the blessing of others. Forget yourself and find someone who needs your service, and you will discover the secret to the happy, fulfilled life. (*The Teachings of Ezra Taft Benson*, ed. Reed A. Benson [Salt Lake City: Bookcraft, 1988], 447, 449)

My experience has been that service to others seldom, if ever, comes at a convenient time. Inevitably, just when your favorite team is playing or your favorite television movie is on, that's when someone needs a blessing or somebody needs help moving. President Spencer W. Kimball has had many things to say about some of the service we can provide and what we can do as individuals to find for ourselves the abundant life. President Kimball likens daily, unselfish service to others as one of the rudimentary mechanics of a successful life. If you only think of yourself and do things for your own development and enjoyment, you will eventually discover that life is not quite what you thought it would be; in fact, you will think life is a bore, and, sadly, you will have lost many friends along your way. You will discover that you have lost the abundant life.

On the other hand, a life dedicated to service and helping our fellow man in whatever capacity is, by all accounts, a life filled with love, inspiration, and example. This is what constitutes the abundant life, as President Kimball states here: "Only when you lift a burden, God will lift your burden. Divine paradox this! *The man who staggers and falls because his burden is too great can lighten that burden by taking on the weight of another's burden.* You get by giving, but your part of giving must be given first" (*The Teachings of Spencer W. Kimball,* ed. Edward L. Kimball [Salt Lake City: Bookcraft, 1982], 251; emphasis added).

In this chapter, we will examine our motives (including the sometimes questionable ones) for performing service. I know that through service we will be able to obtain a change of heart and nurture the seeds that will enable us to have no more desire for sin.

Ten Points to Service

Elder Neal A. Maxwell points out in his book, *All These Things Shall Give Thee Experience* (Salt Lake City: Deseret Book Co., 1979) that Christlike service consists of the following ten points (modified for discussion here). Service to our fellowman can be performed by:

1. Listening genuinely.
2. Receiving righteously, as well as giving.
3. Developing integrity.
4. Willing ourselves to hold back in conversation.
5. Ignoring worries about our own competence.
6. Responding to the achievements of others.
7. Refusing to endorse the seductive slogans of the world.
8. Enduring all things.
9. Offering praise.

10. Bearing the burdens of others.

Listening can be particularly difficult at the end of a hard day, after we get comfortable at home and the drowsiness begins to overtake us. I'm embarrassed to admit that there have been many times when my wife has been talking to me at night over one issue or another, and I have fallen asleep! I know I'm not performing any service to her at that point! By genuinely listening, we can show others that they are important to us and that we are concerned with what they have to say.

If you were to conduct a survey and ask people if it's easier for them to give or to receive, most of them would tell you that it is much easier to give. Receiving, on the other hand, for most of us, is very difficult. Take my own life, for example. I know from personal experience that it is sometimes harder to *receive* than it is to *give*. Most of us love to give, but we often are embarrassed or disgruntled when we are the recipients of service. In the scriptures, a good example of healing and forgiveness that can come from receiving service is the story of Jacob and Esau.

Jacob had received the birthright from his father, Isaac, even though Esau was the eldest. Esau had sold his birthright to Jacob for some bread and pottage in a moment of extreme hunger (see Genesis 25). Several years later, Jacob heard that Esau was in town, and on his way to meet with his elder brother, Jacob put together a gift of several items, including animals (see Genesis 32:13) and took them to his brother. Esau, upon receiving these gifts, learned a very profound lesson. Here is the conversation that followed Jacob's presentation of the gift:

> And he [Esau] said, What meanest thou by all this drove which I met? And he [Jacob] said, These are to find grace in the sight of my lord.
>
> And Esau said, I have enough, my brother; keep that thou hast unto thyself.
>
> And Jacob said, Nay, I pray thee, if now I have found grace in thy sight, then receive my present at my hand: for therefore I have seen thy face, as though I had seen the face of God, and thou wast pleased with me.

Take, I pray thee, my blessing that is brought to thee; because God hath dealt graciously with me, and because I have enough. And he urged him, and he took it." (Genesis 33:8–11)

Here is a situation where some deep-seated animosity was healed and brothers were made whole again. Clearly, Jacob needed to give, and Esau needed to receive. Sometimes in our lives, we will have similar moments when we will need to receive rather than give. Although these are difficult moments, think of the blessings that will come to the giver and the receiver.

Have we ever been jealous of another when something good happens to them? Being supportive of the achievements of others is sometimes not as easy as it sounds. I'm sure we've all seen examples of jealousy and ulterior motive. They are particularly applicable in our vocations. We may find ourselves saying, "Why did Ralph get that promotion instead of me?" or "Why is Joe the golden boy around here? Why can't I have my moment in the sun?" In order to become more Christlike, we need to stretch for that point in our spiritual development where we are *genuinely* excited to hear of the success of others. People are pretty perceptive to artificial encouragement. Learning to be genuine is the challenge we need to work toward to become more Christlike.

My father is a good example of support, encouragement and praise. My wife and I had worked and worked so that I might graduate from college and earn my officer's commission in the U.S. Army, despite all the challenges that came with it. When I was made a second lieutenant, my father was thrilled. He reminded me of how hard we had worked toward this achievement. He acknowledged the sacrifices that my wife and I had endured which made this commissioning more deserving. My father truly understands what genuine happiness for the achievements of others means. Even to this day, he tells me how proud he is of that particular accomplishment in my life.

We can also serve others by enduring well, regardless of circumstances. I believe that our steadiness will steady others who are otherwise on the verge of giving up. This principle is nothing new. In fact it's taught in the scriptures! The Book of Mormon reads, "And there was one day in every week that was set apart that they should gather themselves together to teach the people, and to worship the Lord their God, and also, *as often as it was in their power, to assemble themselves together*" (Mosiah 18:25; emphasis added). We meet together often to help fortify those of us who may need it! There is great strength in numbers, and many times when we are around these others, it helps to strengthen us and hold us up when we are on the verge of giving up or when we have lost hope.

Enduring all things well also makes me think of President Spencer W. Kimball. Here was a man who was intimately familiar with pain and disappointment. His body was constantly ravaged with disease, yet he persisted and embodied the phrase "endure to the end." What a tremendous example he is for us!

By acknowledging my own experiences and hearing about the experiences of others, I have come to know that God will reinforce us and help us after we have made prayerful and wise decisions with regard to serving others. As the Lord said, "When ye are in the service of your fellow beings ye are only in the service of your God" (Mosiah 2:17). Impressions will come to us when we have had time to ponder and reflect on our own behavior. I encourage you to dedicate some time to think and pray about how you have treated others. I know our Father in Heaven will hear each of us and show us ways that we can improve.

From the scriptures, we learn that it is God's work and glory "to bring to pass the immortality and eternal life of man" (Moses 1:39). This is accomplished by using us to further His work. Service to our brothers and sisters is literally the ultimate love. Remember also what the Savior taught us: "Verily I say unto you, Inasmuch as ye have done it unto one of the least of these my brethren, ye have done it unto me" (Matthew 25:40). Remembering these verses in the scriptures will help us to experience the mighty change of heart we want so badly and will allow the Spirit to come into our lives and help us grow from good people to better people.

In one of his First Presidency messages in the *Ensign*, President Gordon B. Hinckley said this:

Generally speaking, the most miserable people I know are those who are obsessed with themselves; the happiest people I know are

103

those who lose themselves in the service of others.... By and large, I have come to see that if we complain about life, it is because we are thinking only of ourselves. For many years there was a sign on the wall of a shoe repair shop I patronized. It read, "I complained because I had no shoes until I saw a man who had no feet." The most effective medicine for the sickness of self-pity is to lose ourselves in the service of others. ("Whosoever Will Save His Life," *Ensign,* August 1982, 5)

Life can be much more valuable and worthwhile if we help others and provide service to those who most need it. What makes life worth living is helping others to help themselves to help others. It is a never-ending cycle for service.

Charity

If we have a problem with service, we need to pray for charity. Charity is the key that unlocks the door to service. Another way to think about this is that service is the key that unlocks the door to charity. Once we truly love somebody, we will only naturally want to serve him or her. Or conversely, once we begin to serve somebody, we will begin to recognize a love for him or her. It is important to realize that we are all brothers and sisters, and, as such, we need to treat each other that way. This realization will help to nourish the seed that puts us on the path toward charity and service.

Like service, charity also has always been an important topic for the Brethren. There are numerous books and inspirational speeches on the subject. Sometimes, during my conversations with others, I feel that we don't fully understand the meaning behind charity. There is so much more to charity than visiting the sick or paying a generous fast offering. Charity is more. It is much more. Elder Marvin J. Ashton has said this about charity:

Real charity is not something you give away; it is something that you acquire and make a part of yourself. And when the virtue of charity becomes implanted in your heart, you are never the same again.

Perhaps the greatest charity comes when we are kind to each other, when we don't judge or categorize someone else, when we simply give each other the benefit of the doubt or remain quiet. Charity is accepting someone's differences, weaknesses, and shortcomings; having patience with someone who has let us down; or resisting the impulse to become offended when someone doesn't handle something the way we might have hoped. ("The Tongue Can Be a Sharp Sword," *Ensign*, May 1992, 19)

The perfect example of charity and service in all things is the Savior, Jesus Christ. He taught us true compassion and perfect love for all mankind. There is no end to the love He has for us or the service He provides through the Atonement. His life was one of unconditional service. We can repay that love through the service that we render here in mortality.

A profound example of charity found in the scriptures that has left an impression with me is the example of the shepherds who were watching over their flock at the time of the Savior's birth. This lesson can be found in the book of Luke. It can easily be overlooked unless we view these verses from the perspective of charity and service. Take a look:

And there were in the same country shepherds abiding in the field, keeping watch over their flock by night.

And, lo, the angel of the Lord came upon them, and the glory of the Lord shone round about them: and they were sore afraid.

And the angel said unto them, Fear not: for, behold, I bring you good tidings of great joy, which shall be to all people.

For unto you is born this day in the city of David a Saviour, which is Christ the Lord.

And this shall be a sign unto you; Ye shall find the babe wrapped in swaddling clothes, lying in a manger.

And suddenly there was with the angel a multitude of the heavenly host praising God, and saying,

Glory to God in the highest, and on earth peace, good will toward men.

And it came to pass, as the angels were gone away from them into heaven, the shepherds said one to another, Let us now go even unto Bethlehem, and see this thing which is come to pass, which the Lord hath made known unto us.

And they came with haste, and found Mary, and Joseph, and the babe lying in a manger. (Luke 2:8–16)

There is a powerful and inspiring message here about charity and service that we can all learn. After this wonderful heavenly manifestation, clearly the shepherds wanted to go to Bethlehem and see for themselves the birth of the Savior. But because of their job, someone had to stay behind to watch the flock! Imagine how difficult it was for the shepherd who stayed behind after seeing that glorious heavenly manifestation and learning that the Savior of the world had just been born a few miles away. I'm positive that the shepherd who did stay behind was blessed for his act of charity and service.

The more service we render, the greater the charity we will have. Service and charity are key elements in the quest to relinquish our natural disposition to do evil and experience a mighty change. We love those we serve. I believe that we are drawn toward people who manifest this quality.

Let me close with the profound words of Elder Maxwell:

Jesus loved us enough to put His own needs in the background in order to better serve others. There was no selfishness about Him, nor any of the "I must meet my needs" philosophy that has seduced and captured so many in our time. Just as He has told us to do, He *found* and *fulfilled* Himself by *losing* himself in the service of others. But we must lose our life *for His sake*—not just any cause. (Neal A. Maxwell, *All These Things Shall Give Thee Experience* [Salt Lake City: Deseret Book Co., 1979] 69; italics in original)

How grateful I am to the people in my life who have taught me that service to my fellow men and women will help me to be able to become more Christlike and allow the Spirit to mold me and help me to experience the mighty change of heart that will transform me from a good person to a better one.

CHAPTER NINE
RECEIVING PERSONAL REVELATION

When I was a young Deacon in the Aaronic Priesthood, I often had the privilege of going home teaching with my father as my companion. One particular month, my dad had been assigned a new sister that he promptly called and obtained an appointment with later in the week. I remember that she was very elderly and a widow. On the appointed day, my father and I drove to the home of this sister. My father told me that all he knew about her was she had been a member all her life; her husband had passed away; she lived on a farm outside of town; and she had been the recipient of service from many in the Ward. I remember how warmly she welcomed us and invited us into her home. After some initial conversation, Dad began the lesson. During that lesson, this sister, who had been a member of the Church her entire life, stopped my father and told him that she had never felt the Spirit of the Lord and could not recall a single spiritual experience in her life. I remember how surprised my father was at hearing that. This sweet sister then asked him how to learn to recognize the Spirit of the Lord. I recall how quiet I was, feeling grateful that my father - and not me - would answer this question, since I did not know the answer yet myself. I was just a kid! I do not remember how my father answered her, but I do remember thinking to myself that I did not want to go through life and have that same difficulty—never learning to recognize the feelings of the Spirit within me.

I have never forgotten this experience. As time goes on, and as I mature in the gospel, I often reflect on how I would respond today if this sweet sister were here to ask me that same question she asked of my father: how to recognize the Spirit of the Lord. What would I tell her now if I was given the chance? What does it mean to feel the Spirit of the Lord? How does one recognize the promptings when they come?

According to the Gospel Topics web page for the Church of Jesus Christ of Latter-day Saints, the term "revelation" is defined as:

"...Communication from God to His children. This guidance comes through various channels according to the needs and circumstances of individuals, families, and the Church as a whole. When the Lord reveals His will to the Church, He speaks through His prophet. Prophets are the only people who can receive revelation for the Church, but they are not the only people who can receive revelation. *According to our faithfulness, we can receive revelation to help us with our specific personal needs, responsibilities, and questions and to help us strengthen our testimony.* (www.lds.org, Gospel Library, Gospel Topics: "Revelation"; emphasis added).

There are many elements to understanding how the Spirit operates and just as many different types of manifestations. For example, as our Father in Heaven's children, we may experience dreams, visions, particular feelings; promptings in one way or another; subtle whisperings of the still small voice giving direction, and so on. We are cautioned in the scriptures to "Trifle not with sacred things." (D&C 6:12) and also to "Remember that that which cometh from above is sacred, and must be spoken with care, and by constraint of the Spirit..."(D&C 63:64). Usually, experiences with the Spirit and specifically with revelation are personal and not to be shared with others unless we feel directed to do so, as they may help someone with a problem that they may be struggling with. Many examples of these kinds of experiences have been recorded for us in the scriptures, and there are many lessons that can be learned from these accounts from the lives of the prophets, (which in my opinion is the reason we know about them).

One example comes from the life of President Brigham Young. At noon on February 17, 1847, as Brigham Young lay ill in bed at Winter

Quarters, he dreamed that he went to see Joseph Smith. After pleading to be reunited with the Prophet and being told that the time was not right, President Young asked if Joseph at least had a word of counsel for the Saints. Brigham Young related:

"Joseph stepped toward me and looking very earnestly, yet pleasantly, said, 'Tell the people to be humble and faithful, and be sure to keep the spirit of the Lord and it will lead them right. Be careful and do not turn away the still small voice; it will teach them what to do and where to go; it will yield the fruits of the kingdom. Tell the brethren to keep their hearts open to conviction, so that when the Holy Ghost comes to them, their hearts will be ready to receive it. They can tell the Spirit of the Lord from all other spirits; it will whisper peace and joy to their souls; it will take malice, strife, and all evil from their hearts, and their whole desire will be to do good, bring forth righteousness and build up the Kingdom of God. Tell the brethren if they will follow the Spirit of the Lord they will go right. Be sure and tell the people to keep the Spirit of the Lord…

Joseph again said, 'Tell the people to be sure and keep the Spirit of the Lord and follow it, and it will lead them just right'" (In Preston Nibley, *Exodus to Greatness* [Salt Lake City: Deseret News Press, 1947], p. 329).

In this particular dream, President Young is told at least four times to follow the Spirit of the Lord, a lesson that conveys just how important it is to follow the Spirit of the Lord.

Revelation comes to us according to the Lord's timetable. We should not put "terms" or timing limits on our Father in Heaven. He will answer us when He feels it is best for us and according to His will. Elder Robert D. Hales of the Quorum of the Twelve Apostles taught the following about revelatory timing:

"Revelation comes on the Lord's timetable, which often means we must move forward in faith, even though we haven't received all the answers we desire. As a General Authority, I was assigned to help reorganize a stake presidency under the direction of Elder Ezra Taft

Benson. After praying, interviewing, studying, and praying again, Elder Benson asked if I knew who the new president would be. I said I had not received that inspiration yet. He looked at me for a long time and replied he hadn't either. However, we *were* inspired to ask three worthy priesthood holders to speak in the Saturday evening session of conference. Moments after the third speaker began, the Spirit prompted me that he should be the new stake president. I looked over at President Benson and saw tears streaming down his face. Revelation had been given to both of us—but only by continuing to seek our Heavenly Father's will as we moved forward in faith."

(Robert D. Hales, "Personal Revelation: "The Teachings and Examples of the Prophets", *Liahona*, November 2007 pg 86-89)

You Will Know It By How You Feel

How does a person know when they truly have received a manifestation of the Holy Ghost? The person will know it by how they *feel*. The Spirit will touch a person to such an extent that they will experience a mighty change of heart and it will change their life forever. President Boyd K. Packer, President of the Quorum of the Twelve Apostles, explained that the "Holy Ghost speaks with a voice that you *feel* more than you *hear*. It is described as a "still small voice." And while we speak of listening to the whisperings of the Spirit, most often one describes a spiritual prompting by saying, "I had a *feeling* …" (Boyd K. Packer, "Personal Revelation: The Gift, the Test, and the Promise", *Ensign*, Nov 1994, pg 59; emphasis added).

A few years ago, the youth of our Stake experienced a handcart trek through Martin's Cove in Wyoming. For three days, they were exposed to the sights, sounds, and feelings associated with this wonderful and sacred area. Prior to leaving, and as the time drew nearer for that event, I remember telling the youth that it's not going to be what they *see*, as much as what they *feel* that will make it special for them. Martin's Cove is not the prettiest location in the world. It is very plain and bleak. Prior to this event, I had heard that if you were not familiar with the history of the events that transpired at Martin's Cove, you could drive right past the site and not give it a moment's notice. At the time I counseled the youth to be aware of what they felt during their visit, they did not understand what I meant. They were anticipating three days of vacation intermingled with a little walking. As stake leaders, we sought to bring this special and sacred part of Church history to life for them. It became an enormous success and the spiritual, faith promoting experiences resulting from this trek helped the youth of our stake when they needed it the most.

As indicated earlier in this book, however, we need to develop our own personal testimony and learn not to rely as much on the experience of others. On one occasion, the Prophet Joseph explained in a response to a request by the twelve apostles for instruction that "reading the experience of others, or the revelation given to *them,* can never give *us* a comprehensive view of our condition and true relation to God" (*History of the Church,* 6:50; emphasis added). This does not mean we should have no interest in Church history or in reading these accounts. My wife and I love LDS Church history and our joy when visiting early Church historical sites is amplified by knowing of their background and studying it beforehand. But the more long lasting spiritual impressions are from *what is felt there, rather than what is remembered.* While visiting the Sacred Grove a few years ago, my wife and I were fortunate enough to find a little private area wherein we pondered the sacred events that had transpired there. It added much to our visit of the site. Both of us came away from this quiet visit uplifted, edified and with our testimonies strengthened.

When we use the scriptures as our primary source of instruction, they abound with such insightful revelatory expressions as: "The veil was taken from our minds, and the eyes of our understanding were opened"(see D&C 110: 1 and Ether 3:6), or "I will tell you in your mind and in your heart" (see D&C 8:2), or "I did enlighten thy mind" (see D&C 6:15 and D&C 11: 13), or "Speak the thoughts that I shall put into your hearts" (see D&C 100: 5), to just name a few. There are literally hundreds of verses of scriptural council which can help us learn of the revelation process. Furthermore, these are all examples of ways that we *feel* more than *hear in the revelatory process.* In the Book of Mormon, Nephi told his wayward brothers, who were visited by an angel, "Ye were past *feeling*, that ye could not *feel* his words" (See 1Nephi 17:45). With the great missionary work we are currently engaged in, missionaries teach investigators and families to identify the Spirit *first*, because teaching them to recognize the Spirit above all other things will help them to understand the truth of what it is they are feeling, and secondly, it will establish this foundation of faith that will help them the rest of their lives.

Elder David A. Bednar of the Quorum of the Twelve Apostles explains this process of learning by faith with the help of the Spirit this way:

"Teaching, exhorting, and explaining, as important as they are, can never convey to an investigator a witness of the truthfulness of the restored gospel. Only as an investigator's faith initiates action and opens the pathway to the heart can the Holy Ghost deliver a confirming witness. Missionaries obviously must learn to teach by the power of the Spirit. Of equal importance, however, is the responsibility missionaries have to help investigators learn by faith" (David A. Bednar, "Seek Learning by Faith", *Ensign*, September 2007, pg 60).

What can create the proper setting or environment so that the Holy Ghost might be sent from heaven to bless the lives of members? It comes by following the scriptures and the teachings of the leaders of the Church. There are many examples of the Holy Ghost manifesting himself in our lives.

How Can The Holy Ghost Help Us?

One way the Holy Ghost helps us is by placing thoughts into our minds. President Marion G. Romney, quoting the prophet Enos, said, "While I was thus struggling in the spirit, behold, the voice of the Lord came into my mind." (see Enos 1:10) Enos then related what the Lord put into his mind. "This", President Romney said, "is a very common means of revelation. It comes into one's mind in words and sentences. With this medium of revelation I am personally well acquainted" (Boyd

K. Packer, "Personal Revelation: The Gift, the Test, and the Promise", *Ensign*, Nov 1994, pg 59).

President Howard W. Hunter (1907-1995) reminded us that obtaining spirituality takes time, patience, and effort: "Developing spirituality ... will not happen by chance, but is accomplished only through deliberate effort and by calling upon God and keeping his commandments" (Howard W. Hunter, "Developing Spirituality", *Ensign*, May, 1979, pg 24). Elder Marion G. Romney (1897-1988) taught us that once we have the Spirit in our lives, we want to assist others to feel the same way: "No person whose soul is illuminated by the burning Spirit of God can ... remain passive. He is driven by an irresistible urge to fit himself to be an active agent of God in *furthering righteousness and in freeing the lives and minds of men from the bondage of sin*" (Conference Report, 4 Oct. 1941, pg 89; emphasis added). In response to a request by the Twelve Apostles for instruction, the prophet Joseph taught, "The best way to obtain truth and wisdom is not to ask it from books, but to go to God in prayer, and obtain divine teaching" (*History of the Church*, 4:425).

A thoughtful quotation I heard once long ago, has resonated in me and really speaks to the truth of the matter: "Always remember that in the Gospel of Jesus Christ, the plan has always been short term discipline and long term happiness. The plan for Satan has always been short term happiness and long term misery". Our Father in Heaven's plan has always been, and always will be, His plan of happiness, not despair. It is a plan of *overwhelming* joy and delight, not devastating bitterness and crushing discontent.

What does a spiritual confirmation feel like? If that elderly sister that my father and I home taught many years ago were here with me now, I would tell her that it's the feeling that comes when you read the Book of Mormon or go to Church. It's the feeling you sense when you go to the Temple or talk of heavenly things to a valued friend. It's the feeling you have when you go to special historic Church sites (like the Sacred Grove) that have been set apart from the rest of the world because of events that have happened there that are so holy and sacred that you want to share it with everybody else. President Boyd K.

Packer, President of the Quorum of the Twelve Apostles spoke clearly about feeling the Spirit when he said:

> "The Holy Ghost communicates with the spirit *through the mind more than through the physical senses.* This guidance comes as *thoughts, as feelings, through impressions and promptings.* It is not always easy to describe inspiration. The scriptures teach us that we may 'feel' the words of spiritual communication more than hear them, and see with spiritual rather than with mortal eyes." (Boyd K. Packer, "Revelation in a Changing World", *Ensign*, Nov 1989, pg 14; emphasis added)

Along these same lines, President Spencer W. Kimball (1895-1985) taught that as we demonstrate to our Father in Heaven our worthiness, in return, our understanding, knowledge, and familiarity of the Holy Ghost will grow with us in time:

> "The gift of the Holy Ghost *grows with worthiness.* If you are baptized when you are eight years old, of course you are a child, and there is much you would not be expected to know. But the Holy Ghost comes to you as you grow and learn and make yourselves worthy. *It comes a little at a time as you merit it. And as your life is in harmony, you gradually receive the Holy Ghost in a great measure.*" (*The Teachings of Spencer W. Kimball*, ed. Edward L. Kimball [Salt Lake City: Bookcraft, 1982], p. 114; emphasis added.)

I feel one of the most important tasks in life is to learn to recognize the gentle promptings of the Holy Ghost and to understand the process of receiving revelation as it pertains to us individually. Perhaps even more importantly, we need to learn to follow the promptings of the Holy Ghost regardless. By following His spirit and allowing that influence in your life, you will find that He can make more of your life than you can.

The following chart has been very helpful for me over the years. As I have aged, I have added to it, so for me, it's a working document:

When you have the Spirit of the Lord with you

1. You feel happy, calm, and clear minded
2. You feel generous
3. Nobody can offend you
4. You wouldn't mind everybody seeing what you are doing
5. You are eager to be with people and want to make them happy
6. You are glad when others succeed
7. You are glad to attend your meetings and participate in church activities
8. You feel like praying
9. You wish you could keep all of the Lord's commandments
10. You feel in control—you don't oversleep too much; you don't feel uncontrollable passions, desires, or lose your temper
11. You think about the Savior often and you want to know Him better
12. You want to serve others

When you don't have the Spirit of the Lord with you

1. You feel unhappy, depressed, confused and frustrated
2. You're possessive, self centered, or resent demands made on you
3. You are easily offended
4. You become sensitive and evasive
5. You avoid people, especially members of your family, and you are critical of family members and church authorities
6. You envy or resent the success of others
7. You don't want to go to Church, go home teaching, or take the sacrament; you wish you had another church job or no job at all
8. You don't want to pray
9. You find the commandments bothersome, restricting, or senseless
10. You feel emotions and appetites so strongly, that you fear you cannot control them—hate, jealousy, anger, lust, hunger, fatigue

11. You hardly ever think of the Savior, He seems irrelevant to your life, or worse part of a confusing system that seems to work against you
12. You get discouraged easily and wonder if life is really worth it

I know that if we find those quiet moments in our life, and we ponder over the events of the day or the week, we will begin to recognize *when* we are being guided by His Spirit and *how* we are being guided by His Spirit. We will be able to put things into proper perspective and really understand the difference between what is most important, and what is not.

CHAPTER TEN
THE FRUITS OF OUR LABORS

What kind of man or woman has been blessed with the disposition to avoid evil and do good continually? Are there any among us today? How can we, as members of The Church of Jesus Christ of Latter-day Saints, do what they do and follow their example? As I think of all these questions, I think of the life of the Savior, for He truly epitomized everything we are so earnestly striving for. Additionally, I think of all the General Authorities, stake presidents, bishops, Sunday School and Primary teachers, and Young Men and Young Women leaders from around the world whom I have gotten to know and to work with over the years. I ponder upon the thousands of Church service and full-time missionaries and think of their powerful example. Not just the young elders and sisters, but the thousands of senior missionary couples who have left behind many of the things that are considered important in the world because of the love they have for their fellow men and their desire to see those people come unto Christ. They do so much and accomplish such great things with little or no recognition. Many of these missionaries, even at much personal sacrifice, have left their entire lives behind to spread the word of the Lord in areas where even the bravest of us would fear to tread! They return to their homes with stories that build our faith and motivate us to do better. These young missionaries leave for a mission at the prime of their lives when dating, playing sports, attending college, and finding careers are what the world considers to be most important. Such experiences may be missed, circumstances and scholarships lost.

Senior missionary couples leave to serve the Lord at a time when retirement, relaxation, vacation, and spending time with grandchildren are considered most important. These people are truly living the word of God. They have experienced a change of heart in their lives and wish to share that with everyone. And there are others, many others, who share the same spirit.

I desire to point out a couple of great people from the scriptures who had the same disposition toward righteousness. Obviously, the Savior is the perfect example. In addition, however, there are some lesser-known examples in the Book of Mormon.

As I mentioned in chapter three, when we think of people from the Book of Mormon, we think of the key figures such as Lehi, Nephi, Alma, Mormon, and Moroni. We think of strong, young, stripling warriors and fantastic accounts of conversion. However, there are many other servants of the Lord found in the pages of the Book of Mormon and other scriptures who have the same qualities and attributes as these well-known servants of the Lord, and each has a mission similar to them as well. Each of these servants is true and faithful to His word and has within their character a desire to share that word to others regardless of the consequences.

Jacob

Jacob, the younger brother of Nephi and son of Lehi, is one such example found in the Book of Mormon of a true and faithful follower of the Lord's word. He is one who personified a change of heart within himself and desired to share that conversion with others.

According to the book of First Nephi, Jacob was born in the wilderness after his family had left Jerusalem and before they had arrived at the promised land (1 Nephi 18:7). Not much is known of his childhood except that his time in the wilderness was a learning experience for young Jacob. A time to see, hear, and feel. A time to be taught by his father, who was a prophet of God. I believe that during this time of youthful development, Jacob acquainted himself with his brother Nephi's teachings and understood them. Jacob saw firsthand how desires, moods, and dispositions can affect someone's spirituality.

It was most likely through the teachings of Nephi and Lehi that he became sensitive to the promptings of the Spirit at an early age and developed a steadfast and immovable testimony.

Jacob was also acquainted with trials and tribulations, which helped prepare him for his future prophetic calling. Because of Jacob's birth in the wilderness, he was probably unaware of his father's prosperity in Jerusalem or the relative comfort that could have come to him had he been born into that environment. Instead, Jacob was familiar with following the Spirit through the example of his father, his brother Nephi, as well as his other righteous older brother, Sam. Jacob was familiar with heartache and sorrow over the behavior of his other brothers, Laman and Lemuel, and also the suffering from hunger, pain, thirst, and other struggles associated with life in the wilderness.

In his early years, Jacob received a patriarchal blessing from his father, Lehi. From that patriarchal blessing we can glean many insights about Jacob's early life:

And now, Jacob, I speak unto you: Thou art my first-born in the days of my tribulation in the wilderness. And behold, in thy childhood thou hast suffered afflictions and much sorrow, because of the rudeness of thy brethren.

Nevertheless, Jacob, my first-born in the wilderness, thou knowest the greatness of God; and he shall consecrate thine afflictions for thy gain.

Wherefore, thy soul shall be blessed, and thou shalt dwell safely with thy brother, Nephi; and thy days shall be spent in the service of thy God. Wherefore, I know that thou art redeemed, because of the righteousness of thy Redeemer; for thou hast beheld that in the fulness of time he cometh to bring salvation unto men.

And thou hast beheld in thy youth his glory; wherefore, thou art blessed even as they unto whom he shall minister in the flesh; for the Spirit is the same, yesterday, today, and forever. And the way is prepared from the fall of man, and salvation is free. (2 Nephi 2:1–4)

Clearly, Jacob had been brought up righteously and had known from an early age what it felt like to have the Savior's influence in his life. This disposition grew stronger and stronger, line upon line, until Jacob, as an older man, grieved exceptionally for the sins of his fellow men. As the prophet and the spiritual leader after the death of Nephi, it physically pained him to have to speak plainly to his brethren about what it was that they were doing wrong in the sight of the Lord. Here he mentions this:

> Yea, it grieveth my soul and causeth me to shrink with shame before the presence of my Maker, that I must testify unto you concerning the wickedness of your hearts.
>
> And also it grieveth me that I must use so much boldness of speech concerning you, before your wives and your children, many of whose feelings are exceedingly tender and chaste and delicate before God, which thing is pleasing unto God. (Jacob 2:6–7)

Further on, toward the end of the second chapter of Jacob, he adds the following:

> And now behold, my brethren, ye know that these commandments were given to our father, Lehi; wherefore, ye have known them before; and ye have come unto great condemnation; for ye have done these things which ye ought not to have done.
>
> Behold, ye have done greater iniquities than the Lamanites, our brethren. Ye have broken the hearts of your tender wives, and lost the confidence of your children, because of your bad examples before them; and the sobbings of their hearts ascend up to God against you. And because of the strictness of the word of God, which cometh down against you, many hearts died, pierced with deep wounds. (Jacob 2:34–35)

Here is a man who was truly not afraid to call it like it was. He did not pad anything because he was afraid of hurting someone's feelings. He was bold, powerful, and full of the Spirit. This is a man who has truly abandoned his disposition to do evil and instead has chosen to do good only. Jacob understood the power of teaching by example then following up to make sure that everybody understood. He genuinely loved his fellow men, and I think this attribute was the driver that helped to change his people's dispositions. Jacob was unshakable in his faith and could not be persuaded in any other direction (see Jacob 4:18).

All of these qualities helped Jacob influence his people toward goodness when they were faced with a severe trial of their faith against the anti-Christ, Sherem. Jacob tells us this about Sherem:

> And now it came to pass after some years had passed away, there came a man among the people of Nephi, whose name was Sherem.
>
> And it came to pass that he began to preach among the people, and to declare unto them that there should be no Christ. And he preached many things which were flattering unto the people; and this he did that he might overthrow the doctrine of Christ.
>
> And he labored diligently that he might lead away the hearts of the people, insomuch that he did lead away many hearts; and he knowing that I, Jacob, had faith in Christ who should come, he sought much opportunity that he might come unto me.
>
> And he was learned, that he had a perfect knowledge of the language of the people; wherefore, he could use much flattery, and much power of speech, according to the power of the devil. (Jacob 7:1–4)

In earlier chapters, I have indicated that I have met some of these people who were perfect in the "knowledge of the language of the people" and who desired to tear down our testimonies of the restored gospel of Jesus Christ. Bringing ourselves into this cynical environment is an extremely frightening situation and should be avoided at all costs. If we listen to these people long enough, eventually we will begin to question our own testimony and find ourselves at the exact fork in the road where the adversary wants us, where he can be given the opportunity to sway us onto the wrong path.

Not only did Jacob confront this anti-Christ, but, with the help of the Spirit, he got Sherem to admit the errors of his ways and retract the teaching that he had been offering the people. What an incredible accomplishment! Armed only with the power of the Lord, Jacob confronted this anti-Christ:

Behold, the Lord God poured in his Spirit into my soul, insomuch that I did confound him in all his words.

And I said unto him: Deniest thou the Christ who shall come? And he said: If there should be a Christ, I would not deny him; but I know that there is no Christ, neither has been, nor ever will be.

And I said unto him: Believest thou the scriptures? And he said, Yea. (Jacob 7: 8–10)

In the next verse, pay special attention to how Jacob responds to Sherem:

And I said unto him: Then ye do not understand them; for they truly testify of Christ. Behold, I say unto you that none of the prophets have written, nor prophesied, save they have spoken concerning this Christ. (Jacob 7:11)

How many of us have the courage to bear strong testimony about the gospel of Jesus Christ to someone who mocks our beliefs or who is eloquent in language or especially educated? For Jacob to be as bold as to say to Sherem, *"ye do not understand them,"* is absolutely fascinating to me. We will discover that later on Jacob also tells Sherem that he is of the devil. Could we say that to the face of our antagonist, our rival, or temptation? Do we have that kind of divine courage? Jacob continues interrogating Sherem thus:

And this is not all—it has been made manifest unto me, for I have heard and seen; and it also has been made manifest unto me by the power of the Holy Ghost; wherefore, I know if there should be no atonement made all mankind must be lost.

And it came to pass that he said unto me: Show me a sign by this power of the Holy Ghost, in the which ye know so much.

And I said unto him: What am I that I should tempt God to show unto thee a sign in the thing which thou knowest to be true? Yet thou wilt deny it, because thou art of the devil. Nevertheless, not my will be done; but if God shall smite thee, let that be a sign unto thee that he has power, both in heaven and in earth; and also, that Christ shall come. And thy will, O Lord, be done, and not mine.

And it came to pass that when I, Jacob, had spoken these words, the power of the Lord came upon him, insomuch that he fell to the earth. And it came to pass that he was nourished for the space of many days.

And it came to pass that he said unto the people: Gather together on the morrow, for I shall die; wherefore, I desire to speak unto the people before I shall die.

And it came to pass that on the morrow the multitude were gathered together; and he spake plainly unto them and denied the things which he had taught them, and confessed the Christ, and the power of the Holy Ghost, and the ministering of angels.

And he spake plainly unto them, that he had been deceived by the power of the devil. And he spake of hell, and of eternity, and of eternal punishment.

And he said: I fear lest I have committed the unpardonable sin, for I have lied unto God; for I denied the Christ, and said that I believed the scriptures; and they truly testify of him. And because I have thus lied unto God I greatly fear lest my case shall be awful; but I confess unto God.

And it came to pass that when he had said these words he could say no more, and he gave up the ghost.

And when the multitude had witnessed that he spake these things as he was about to give up the ghost, they were astonished exceedingly; insomuch that the power of God came down upon them, and they were overcome that they fell to the earth. (Jacob 7:12–21)

Can you imagine how Jacob must have felt at this point? When Sherem told Jacob to gather the people together so that he could inform them how he had misled them, Jacob was probably pleased. The moment had arrived that Jacob had been praying for, when he was able to teach the people with the right frame of mind. The people were ready to hear, and thus the "love of God was restored again among the people" (see Jacob 7:23).

The closer we live to the Spirit, the more we learn to genuinely love the people with whom we associate, despite whatever hardships we may have to endure. Jacob is a person who unquestionably lived close to the Spirit and, as a result, loved his people with true Christlike love. Because of his overwhelming *love* for his people, his *desire* to *obey* and *please* our Father in Heaven, his unquestionable *courage,* and his unswerving *faith*, Jacob was truly a man who had experienced a mighty change and had gone from being a good person to a better one. One that we should all emulate.

Abinadi

Like Jacob, Abinadi too displayed this tremendous love for the people he was sent to teach and encourage in the face of extreme adversity. Unfortunately, little is known about his early years or his place of origin. As far as we know, Abinadi could have even been a convert to the Church.

Abinadi makes his entrance onto the pages of the Book of Mormon by way of a simple statement: "And it came to pass that there was a man among them whose name was Abinadi; and he went forth among them, and began to prophesy, saying: Behold, thus saith the Lord, and thus hath he commanded me, saying, Go forth, and say unto this people, thus saith the Lord—Wo be unto this people, for I have seen their abominations, and their wickedness, and their whoredoms; and except they repent I will visit them in mine anger" (Mosiah 11:20).

It is assumed, then, that Abinadi was brought up in righteousness and was familiar with the teachings of Jesus Christ. He was well enough acquainted with the Spirit that he understood the workings of the Spirit upon him and was able to be used as a mouthpiece for the Lord in preaching repentance unto the people. Upon his entry into the Book of Mormon, he had already been prepared and tutored in what it was that he needed to do. Clearly, Abinadi was the authorized mouthpiece of the Lord. However, in this particular place, King Noah's domain, it is not clear whether Abinadi was intimately known to any of the people or not. We read further on that King Noah had not heard of him or, possibly, felt judged by him:

Now when king Noah had heard of the words which Abinadi had spoken unto the people, he was also wroth; and he said: Who is Abinadi, that I and my people should be judged of him, or who is the Lord, that shall bring upon my people such great affliction?

I command you to bring Abinadi hither, that I may slay him, for he has said these things that he might stir up my people to anger one with another, and to raise contentions among my people; therefore I will slay him.

Now the eyes of the people were blinded; therefore they hardened their hearts against the words of Abinadi, and they sought from that time forward to take him. And king Noah hardened his heart against the word of the Lord, and he did not repent of his evil doings. (Mosiah 11:27–29)

At this point, Abinadi had to leave the area despite whatever success he was having. There is no record of where he went or what he did for the next two years. Perhaps he went on another mission or perhaps he received more spiritual education. What we do know is that Abinadi went back after a two-year leave of absence in disguise to again preach the word of God to this people. Mosiah chapter eleven tells us many things. Among them are these points:

1. Apparently Abinadi was so successful in his first mission with getting his message heard that it caused much commotion and the people in authority wanted him killed (See Mosiah 11:29). If he wasn't so successful about getting his message out, I don't believe he would have needed to come back in disguise.
2. Perhaps most important is the fact that, clearly, Father in Heaven loves his people so much that He is willing to send his designated messengers into these cities despite their bad reception to these servants of the Lord. Our Father in Heaven gives His children chance after chance after chance to come back into His fold. Do we as parents ever give up on our children? If we are loving parents, the answer to that question is a resounding "no!"

3. Imagine how much courage it must have taken to come back after the initial assassination attempt (or attempts) failed and Abinadi left the city! He must still have been wanted by King Noah's officials or else there would have been no need for him to be disguised.

Clearly, Abinadi knew the potential risks to his life by coming back. There is no mention made about how Abinadi prepared for his return, but he did return, despite the possible repercussions. He was obedient and faithful, knowing full well that his life was in danger. Here is where the story of Abinadi gets even more interesting. It was at this point, upon Abinadi's re-entry into the city and his continued attempts to teach the word of the Lord to the people, that King Noah had Abinadi cast into prison. Abinadi was then brought to the chamber where the priests of King Noah began to question him. However, Abinadi cleverly turns the tables on the priests and begins to question them! He successfully moves from hostile witness to powerful interrogator! These are the words he spoke to the priests:

> And now Abinadi said unto them: Are you priests, and pretend to teach this people, and to understand the spirit of prophesying, and yet desire to know of me what these things mean?
>
> I say unto you, wo be unto you for perverting the ways of the Lord! For if ye understand these things ye have not taught them; therefore, ye have perverted the ways of the Lord.
>
> Ye have not applied your hearts to understanding; therefore, ye have not been wise. Therefore, what teach ye this people? (Mosiah 12:25–27)

What tremendous courage this must have taken! How painful it must have been for the priests to hear this reproof coming from someone they had just arrested for stirring up the people and causing commotion!

There is a degree of arrogance in the priests' response as the inquisition continues:

And they said: We teach the law of Moses.

And again he said unto them: If ye teach the law of Moses why do ye not keep it? Why do ye set your hearts upon riches? Why do ye commit whoredoms and spend your strength with harlots, yea, and cause this people to commit sin, that the Lord has cause to send me to prophesy against this people, yea, even a great evil against this people?

Know ye not that I speak the truth? Yea, ye know that I speak the truth; and you ought to tremble before God. (Mosiah 12:28–30)

What magnificence! What beautiful boldness spoken to a group of people who clearly prided themselves in the fact that they were priests of the king and believed that they knew more than the common folk. They believed they were more spiritual than anybody else. They believed that because they had the favor of the king, they were untouchable. Now, here comes this Abinadi and tells them otherwise. I believe that this bold and divine assertiveness from Abinadi was necessary in order to get Alma to change his thinking. These wicked priests were so upset with this turn of events and the message that Abinadi was delivering that they attempted again to kill him. The Book of Mormon continues thus:

And now when the king had heard these words, he said unto his priests: Away with this fellow, and slay him; for what have we to do with him, for he is mad.

And they stood forth and attempted to lay their hands on him; but he withstood them, and said unto them:

Touch me not, for God shall smite you if ye lay your hands upon me, for I have not delivered the message which the Lord sent me to deliver; neither have I told you that which ye requested that I should tell; therefore, God will not suffer that I shall be destroyed at this time.

But I must fulfil the commandments wherewith God has commanded me; and because I have told you the truth ye are angry with me. And again, because I have spoken the word of God ye have judged me that I am mad.

Now it came to pass after Abinadi had spoken these words that the people of king Noah durst not lay their hands on him, for the Spirit of the Lord was upon him; and his face shone with exceeding luster, even as Moses' did while in the mount of Sinai, while speaking with the Lord. (Mosiah 13:1–5)

After giving a powerful discourse, Abinadi again is bound and taken to prison. Clearly, Abinadi had *some* influence over the court because Alma believed the words of Abinadi and was "cast out from among them" (Mosiah 17:3). It took King Noah and the other priests three days of consultation before they were able to agree upon a sentencing.

And after three days, having counseled with his priests, he caused that he [Abinadi] should again be brought before him.

And he said unto him: Abinadi, we have found an accusation against thee, and thou art worthy of death. (Mosiah 17:6–7)

Imagine how Abinadi must have felt at this point. His death had just been pronounced upon him. I believe that the ultimate test of his faith came at this point. What would most of us do? How would we react? Would we still be able to genuinely love the people whom the Lord had sent us to convert? Because of Abinadi's divine nature and his disposition, failure was *not* an option. Here was Abinadi's test:

For thou hast said that God himself should come down among the children of men; and now, for this cause thou shalt be put to death unless thou wilt recall all the words which thou hast spoken evil concerning me and my people. (Mosiah 17:8)

A window of opportunity was made available to Abinadi. He did not acquiesce. He did not yield. He would triumph over his foes by his divine answer. This was how Abinadi answered:

Now Abinadi said unto him: I say unto you, I will not recall the words which I have spoken unto you concerning this people, for they are true; and that ye may know of their surety I have suffered myself that I have fallen into your hands.

Yea, and I will suffer even until death, and I will not recall my words, and they shall stand as a testimony against you. And if ye slay me ye will shed innocent blood, and this shall also stand as a testimony against you at the last day. (Mosiah 17: 9–10)

In his moment of trial, Abinadi was triumphant because of his pronouncement of strength, integrity, and faith in God. He was again taken and bound, tortured, and martyred for his beliefs. Here is the scene of his final suffering:

And it came to pass that they took him and bound him, and scourged his skin with faggots, yea, even unto death.

And now when the flames began to scorch him, he cried unto them, saying:

Behold, even as ye have done unto me, so shall it come to pass that thy seed shall cause that many shall suffer the pains that I do suffer, even the pains of death by fire; and this because they believe in the salvation of the Lord their God.

And it will come to pass that ye shall be afflicted with all manner of diseases because of your iniquities.

Yea, and ye shall be smitten on every hand, and shall be driven and scattered to and fro, even as a wild flock is driven by wild and ferocious beasts.

And in that day ye shall be hunted, and ye shall be taken by the hand of your enemies, and then ye shall suffer, as I suffer, the pains of death by fire.

Thus God executeth vengeance upon those that destroy his people. O God, receive my soul.

And now, when Abinadi had said these words, he fell, having suffered death by fire; yea, having been put to death because he would not deny the commandments of God, having sealed the truth of his words by his death. (Mosiah 17:13–20)

Like his predecessor, the prophet Jacob, Abinadi displayed all the divine qualities inherent in the true followers of Christ, those who wish to do only good and repel all evil, those who wish to experience a change of heart and go from good to better. It takes great strength of character. Clearly, Abinadi had enough love for his Father in Heaven and for the people he wanted so badly to convert to the gospel of Jesus Christ to willingly put himself through so much trauma and tribulation. Nobody enjoys being ridiculed. Imagine how it must feel to know you are going to be killed. Imagine how our own Lord and Savior Jesus Christ must have felt during His final hours in mortality.

I started this chapter off mentioning a little about the dispositions of the General Authorities and the numerous bishops, stake presidents, Sunday School and Primary teachers, Young Men and Young Women leaders in the Church around the world who have the same disposition that Jacob and Abinadi displayed. Although our sacrifices today aren't usually as drastic, it still takes tremendous courage and devotion to remain true to your principles and have a firm faith in the gospel. We can still love others as Christ would love us, as these great examples have demonstrated. The rewards are the fruits of our labors.

It is these people I honor: the people who say no when they are offered alcoholic beverages at a party; the people who say "I don't think so" when they are confronted with pornography; the people who avoid seeing R-rated movies when everyone else around them is telling them that "it's okay" and that it's a wonderful movie despite its rating. People who keep the Sabbath day holy despite what the world may be doing around them. It takes tremendous courage to persist and continue to proselytize when doors are being slammed in your face and you are being mocked and ridiculed for your beliefs. These are the people who are the real heroes—the silent warriors who continue to hold fast despite all the tribulations that come to them, the people who perform invisible acts of service to make a difference in other's lives, the people who show love and compassion to rejected members of society, the people who endure to the end and persevere despite life's obstacles, the people who quell their natural disposition to do evil and use their potential for good. They are the people who have accepted the challenge and gone from good to better. And the glowing embers of their hearts draw us to them because they are celestial. They are the ones who can help us all experience a change of heart, and they are all around us. How grateful I am for these people!

As the old saying goes, we must be on higher ground ourselves if we are to lift others. I submit to you that we are inherently drawn toward these kinds of people because they are celestial and can help us to lift ourselves and to become better people.

EPILOGUE

In order to have the disposition to run from any wrongdoing or evil, it is essential that we are obedient to *all* the commandments of our Father in Heaven. In our quest to have this disposition, we may often experience much criticism and ridicule, even from others who believe as we do and who may secretly respect us for doing the right thing. It is not enough for us to know what is right and to believe it is good. We must take a stand and be willing to be counted among those in the scriptures like Jacob, Abinadi, and Enos, who have marked the way for us. We must be willing to act in accordance with what we believe under all circumstances. We cannot serve two masters in this life (see Matthew 6:24). We cannot be fence-sitters. It takes tremendous courage in today's world to be a devout member of The Church of Jesus Christ of Latter-day Saints. For many of us, being a member of this church is not easy, and it will likely not become easier. It isn't supposed to. The gospel of Jesus Christ is of little value to us if we behave contrary to it. It is important for us to always remember that even the Savior was ignored and at times tormented, ridiculed, spat upon, and eventually crucified because He would not waver in His convictions. Certainly, His was not an easy life.

On entering the waters of baptism, we entered an agreement to take the Lord's name upon us and to always remember Him. If we are an endowed member of the Church, we made certain covenants in the temple, which help us. All we have to do is keep our word. To disobey would be to betray the decision and commitment we have already made. President Howard W. Hunter once said:

The supreme test [of life] is our willingness to be totally obedient. Are we willing to become totally obedient to God's law? There comes a time in our lives when a definite decision must be made. Obedience is not tested when life is calm and pleasant and when we are deriving spiritual satisfaction from doing good; but when thoughts or pressures persuade us to act in a way contrary to God's commandments, then obedience is put to the test. (*The Teachings of Howard W. Hunter*, ed. Clyde J. Williams [Salt Lake City: Bookcraft, 1997], 24)

The servants of God in every age have taught the importance of true compliance to His laws. We must first know for ourselves that the gospel is true, then desire to change the way we behave and have that change manifest itself in us through the Spirit. Heber C. Kimball once said, "The time will come when no man or woman will be able to stand on borrowed light. Each of you will have to be guided with the light within himself. If you do not have it, how can you stand?" (Orson F. Whitney, *The Life of Heber C. Kimball* [Salt Lake City: Deseret Book Co.] n.d., 449–450).

In order to get to this point where we don't have to rely on other people's light, I suggest these following five steps:

1. *Know what we want.* When we hear our leaders in general conference or when we associate with others who have already achieved the mighty change, we need to look to them for guidance. We need to want to be like them, so that we can enjoy what they enjoy. We need to want to radiate the Spirit like they do.

2. *Know what we have to give.* We must earnestly strive and desire to have our natural disposition changed. Such an integral change requires sincere prayer, fasting and willingness to serve others regardless of assignment. We need to endure our trials of faith so that we may sit as equals with Job, Abraham, Joseph Smith, and others who have endured to the end and paved the way before us. We need to repent and let the Atonement become part of our lives. We need to stay away from gossiping and

backbiting of any sort. We need to look to the scriptures and follow the example of others who have overcome their disposition to do evil and have gone from good to better.

3. *Know what others have to give.* To get to the point where we have eliminated our natural disposition to do evil, we need to associate ourselves with others who believe as we do. Chances are, we won't find them frequenting porn shops, gambling casinos, or gossiping over a cup of coffee. We will find these people attending church, doing all the things our Father in Heaven wants them to do, and doing them to the best of their ability.

4. *Pay attention to the little things.* As we have discussed previously, our faith is built precept by precept and can grow to become extremely powerful. Everything we do in the Church is based on our faith that we will be blessed for our efforts. Wouldn't it be a shame to live ninety-nine percent of the gospel and miss out on that one percent that might make the difference between achieving the mighty change and failing at it? We need to serve God with complete integrity, even in the small things. The small things will lead us to the big things.

5. *Stay the course.* As President Spencer W. Kimball has said many times during his tenure as our leader, "endure to the end and lengthen your stride." This is the most difficult aspect of true righteousness. The Lord does not want us to be quitters, in spite of all the wickedness and opposition in the world. We need to have the courage to endure, stay the course, and be counted as true, devoted followers of Christ.

Our beloved prophet provides leadership. He is a guidepost for any issue or question we may have. He receives his inspiration from Jesus Christ, who stands as the "chief cornerstone" of this great work today (Ephesians 2:20). We should never be worried or confused about which path to take. The correct way has been presented to us; we can find it by reading the word of the Lord and listening to Him speak through his ordained representatives. One of our former prophets, President Ezra Taft Benson, once said:

Latter-day Saints should not become bewildered. They should not become worried. They should not become confused in this great and modern world in which we live, with the great changes which are taking place, *because we can have an anchor in these eternal principles and verities which should always bring to us the answer to the problems which face us from day to day.* This is true whether it be a problem involving government, whether it be a problem involving us in business, whether it be some moral issue or some economic issue, we have the guide for the answer to these problems in the eternal principles that have been revealed and are set forth in holy writ and are given to us by the priesthood of God from the lips of those who preside in the earth in the day in which we live. (*The Teachings of Ezra Taft Benson*, ed. Reed A. Benson [Salt Lake City: Bookcraft, 1988], 332; emphasis added)

It takes time, reflection, consideration, and often some diligent questioning. But the mighty change can come and will come line upon line, precept upon precept. Desire is the key, followed closely behind by action. We have discussed many aspects of gospel living that will contribute to our disposition to do no more evil. As we live these higher principles, we are establishing for ourselves a firm foundation (see Matthew 7: 24–27).

The process of gaining spirituality and changing our natural disposition can be compared to dieting in order to lose weight. Both require work, effort, and tremendous self-control. When we start to diet, we often have strong cravings for the foods we used to eat—especially at night and when we are alone and away from any external motivation. In similar fashion, you will find that as you begin to exercise your spirituality in order to overcome the disposition to do evil, temptations to revert to old behaviors will give you trouble at first. Satan will put obstacles in your path to distract you from the goal and make you want to give up. It's not easy, but anything worth getting is worth working hard for. A friend of mine has a print of the Savior on his wall that says "I never said it would be easy, I only said it would be worth it." The question is, do we want to put forth the effort that will make our lives worth living at their utmost potential? A key eternal truth to remember is that Satan's plan will always be short-term happiness and long-term misery. The gospel of Jesus Christ has always been, and will continue to be, short-term discipline and long-term happiness.

President Harold B. Lee once said this about the effort we put into our spiritual development:

> We must train our spiritual selves with the same care, if we are to be fully developed, as we train our physical bodies. We must have daily exercise by our spirits by prayer, by doing daily good deeds, by sharing with others. We must feed our spirits daily by studying the scriptures every day, by [family home evening], by attendance at meetings, by the partaking of the sacrament .... Our spiritual checkups are when we are brought face-to-face with God's spiritual doctors—our bishops, our stake presidents, and occasionally with the General Authorities in interviews, which are always done for the purpose of helping to prepare us for spiritual advancement. (*The Teachings of Harold B. Lee,* ed. Clyde J. Williams [Salt Lake City: Bookcraft, 1996], 122; brackets in original)

With the help of these great men and women to whom the Lord has given leadership assignments, we can grow and continue to develop to the point that we literally have no more disposition to do evil but good only. We can experience this mighty change within ourselves. Personal Priesthood Interviews (PPIs) and the temple recommend questions should be something to look forward to, a chance to give accountability of our lives to the Lord's anointed. How grateful I am for these wonderful examples to me, not just the examples from the scriptures, but also the men and women from today who earnestly strive each day to lift us all to a higher level and who are not satisfied with anything less than the best that is in us. May the time come in our own lives when we do as the people of King Benjamin did:

> They all cried with one voice, saying: Yea, we believe all the words which thou hast spoken unto us; and also, we know of their surety and truth, because of the Spirit of the Lord Omnipotent, which has

wrought a mighty change in us, or in our hearts, that we have no more disposition to do evil, but to do good continually.

And we, ourselves, also, through the infinite goodness of God, and the manifestations of his Spirit, have great views of that which is to come; and were it expedient, we could prophesy of all things.

And it is the faith which we have had on the things which our king has spoken unto us that has brought us to this great knowledge, whereby we do rejoice with such exceedingly great joy.

And we are willing to enter into a covenant with our God to do his will, and to be obedient to his commandments in all things that he shall command us, all the remainder of our days, that we may not bring upon ourselves a never-ending torment, as has been spoken by the angel, that we may not drink out of the cup of the wrath of God. (Mosiah 5:2–5)

How grateful I am for parents, Primary teachers, Sunday School teachers, seminary teachers, all the Young Men and Young Women leaders, Relief Society sisters, missionaries from around the world, and all the other leaders and workers in the Church who help us every day to develop our spirituality. I know that we can make it! Our Father in Heaven loves us and wants us to be with Him for eternity. He speaks to His anointed, so by hearing them, we have heard God's word. We need only follow it to return to live with Him.

Each of us is a participant in a great adventure. We live in the final dispensation, the dispensation of the fullness of times. Such a great opportunity and blessing has been afforded to us! There are multitudes of people beyond the veil, unseen to us, who, even today, are cheering us on every step of the way. There is no room for mediocrity, complacency or spiritual atrophy. There is too much at stake. I once heard an old saying that can refer to getting to the celestial kingdom: "It's easy if you work at it hard, and hard if you work at it easy." Very true words, indeed!

We can make it! We can do it! Let us strive to fulfill our potential and live our lives in accordance with the Savior's teachings. We can be happy. It is His promise. We just need to realize our part of the bargain.

It is my earnest prayer that we can learn from the scriptures and from the great people around us and achieve the change of heart necessary to become better people and live our lives in harmony with His plan for us.

About the Author

Christopher R. Greenwood served an LDS Church mission in Brisbane, Australia and has attended California State University, Sacramento and the U.S. Army Logistics Management College in Virginia. He and his wife, Tami, have five children and are currently living in Utah.